TABLE OF CONTENTS

Top 20 Test Taking Tips

1. Carefully follow all the test registration procedures
2. Know the test directions, duration, topics, question types, how many questions
3. Setup a flexible study schedule at least 3-4 weeks before test day
4. Study during the time of day you are most alert, relaxed, and stress free
5. Maximize your learning style; visual learner use visual study aids, auditory learner use auditory study aids
6. Focus on your weakest knowledge base
7. Find a study partner to review with and help clarify questions
8. Practice, practice, practice
9. Get a good night's sleep; don't try to cram the night before the test
10. Eat a well balanced meal
11. Know the exact physical location of the testing site; drive the route to the site prior to test day
12. Bring a set of ear plugs; the testing center could be noisy
13. Wear comfortable, loose fitting, layered clothing to the testing center; prepare for it to be either cold or hot during the test
14. Bring at least 2 current forms of ID to the testing center
15. Arrive to the test early; be prepared to wait and be patient
16. Eliminate the obviously wrong answer choices, then guess the first remaining choice
17. Pace yourself; don't rush, but keep working and move on if you get stuck
18. Maintain a positive attitude even if the test is going poorly
19. Keep your first answer unless you are positive it is wrong
20. Check your work, don't make a careless mistake

Foundations, Characteristics, and Assessment

Social-emotional development

The stages of Erikson's social-emotional development are:

- Learning Basic Trust vs. Basic Mistrust: The period of infancy in the first years of life where children who are loved and cared for develop trust and security. Children who are not become mistrustful and insecure.
- Learning Autonomy vs. Shame: This occurs during early childhood, where the well-loved child welcomes his new sense of control, manifesting itself in tantrums, possessiveness, and the "no" and "mine" stage.
- Learning Initiative vs. Guilt: A healthy child, usually up to school age, will develop his imagination, cooperate with others, and be both a leader and follower. A child who feels guilt will be fearful, not quite fit in socially, be dependent on adults, and have an underdeveloped imagination.
- Industry vs. Inferiority: Entering school and up to junior high, the child will learn formal skills of life, initiate rules into free play, and desire self-discipline.
- Learning Identity vs. Identity Diffusion: From adolescence to late teens, the child answers the question as to who he is, after possibly going through rebellions and self-doubt. He may experiment with different roles, but anticipate achievement instead of feeling paralyzed by this process.
- Learning Intimacy vs. Isolation: A successful young adult pursues true intimacy, whether it is in the form of long-lasting and enduring friendships or a partner for marriage.
- Learning Generativity vs. Self-Absorption: Once adulthood is reached, whether in marriage or parenthood, the sense of working cooperatively and productively becomes of the utmost importance, rather than focusing only on independent goals.
- Integrity vs. Despair: Once all other seven steps have been resolved, the mature adult reaches adjustment integrity. He can experiment after working hard and has developed a self-concept of which makes him happy and is proud of what he has created.

Cognitive learning

Cognitive approaches to learning focus on emphasizing ways to enhance students' intrinsic nature to make sense of the world around them. Students do this by learning and organizing information, problem-solving and finally developing the concepts and language in order to convey what they see. It refers to the way that students process information. The style in which one learns is described as a dimension of one's personality. Attitudes, values, and social interactions are all dimensions of these influences. Once a teacher has an idea of the cognitive learning styles of his students, he can better gauge how to direct the information at them. He may find that one of his classes does much better with small group work, whereas another group works more effectively individually. There will always be a wide range of ability in any class, and getting to know the students' styles is always going to be effective.

Learning styles

The different learning styles that affect how students learn and perform are:

- Visual learners—These students learn best by seeing written directions and benefit from having notes written down on a whiteboard or overhead. They are able to extract information from written text well and benefit from having main points summarized on the board during class discussions.
- Oral learners—These students perform better when information can be heard; for instance, they may prefer to read aloud or listen to someone else read aloud. Discussions can be helpful in order to hear the information once, and then repeat it to someone else.
- Kinesthetic learners—These students benefit from hands-on experiences and learn best from participating in the classroom, such as conducting a science experiment.

Multiple intelligences

Howard Gardner outlines eight distinct intelligences that people use in problem solving: namely, linguistic, musical, logical-mathematical, spatial, bodily-kinesthetic, naturalistic, interpersonal and intrapersonal, with a possible ninth: existential. Schools traditionally emphasize linguistic and logical-mathematical. Gardner placed emphasis upon learning skills in context, such as apprenticeships, rather than solely by textbooks. Traditional subjects, like English and math, should be taught in ways that appeal to all the multiple intelligences. History, for example, could be taught through dramatic reenactments, biographies, and architecture. He also thought that assessments should be tailored to different abilities and that student choice with assessments would ensure that the students were completing the task to the best of their abilities and utilizing the intelligence in which they were most skilled.

Gender differences

Many observational studies have found that girls are treated differently than boys in the classroom setting; more often to the girls' detriment. This is primarily because males tend to have more interaction with the teachers as their behavior is more assertive and they tend to dominate class discussions, whereas females tend to sit quietly and be passive. Boys tend to call out and are encouraged to participate, but when girls call out, their behavior is corrected and they are more likely to be called on if they raise their hands. Teachers also exhibit lower expectations for girls in classes such as math and science. Despite these issues, girls are tending to do better in school overall, except mainly in issues of self-esteem, of which boys tend to have much higher levels when high school is completed.

The steps teachers can take to address the inequities between how girls and boys are treated in their classrooms are as follows:

- Being metacognitive of the way they deal with girls and boys differently
- Ensuring that boys and girls are not segregating themselves in the classroom by having a mixed seating plan. Having a seating plan that alternates boy-girl-boy-girl can also be an effective classroom management tool.
- Checking resources, such as textbooks and videos, to make sure that both sexes are represented equally in a variety of roles. If there is a textbook or video that has a gender bias, it can be used to spark a conversation on the topic.
- Planning activities so that both sexes have an equal opportunity to

participate, such as rewarding those students who raise their hands before calling out.

- Having a classroom culture, and more importantly, a school culture, that does not tolerate gender bias.

Cultural differences

The cultural differences that might affect behavior include: eye contact, hand movements, silence, religious belief and loss of face. It is important to know the differences that some students may have with eye contact; for example, in some cultures, looking down is seen as a sign of disrespect, whereas with some students that is the way to show respect and that they are paying attention. Some students may laugh or smile out of nervousness when under pressure, falsely leading teachers to assume that they are being rude or misbehaving. Silence is one that varies between genders and cultures. Girls tend to be quieter, and students who are silent when called upon could actually be waiting for more direction instead of the impression that they are not paying attention. Religious beliefs come into effect when doing particular activities that certain religions would find inappropriate, therefore causing students to be reluctant to participate, not because they don't know what to do but because they cannot do the activity.

Special needs students

Qualifying disabilities

The various types of disabilities that qualify individuals for special education programs include specific learning disabilities, speech or language impairments, intellectual disabilities, emotional disturbance, multiple disabilities, hearing impairments, orthopedic impairments, visual impairments, autism, combined deafness and blindness, traumatic brain injury, and other health impairments. Students are classified under one of the categories, and special education teachers are prepared to work with specific groups. Early identification of a child with special needs is an important part of a special education teacher's job. Early intervention is essential in educating children with disabilities.

Handling needs of disabled students

The most important thing to remember is to not stereotype students solely because of their appearance. A student in a wheelchair does not automatically have a learning disability, merely because his physical disability is more apparent, whereas a student with intellectual disabilities may require repetition in order to master the most simple of tasks. Students with disabilities may be in your classroom for varying amounts of time during the day. Making use of the special education staff in your school to familiarize yourselves with the abilities of your students will enable you to assist them to the best of their abilities in your classroom. Ultimately, they are treated as you would treat any student. You need to assess their abilities, finding their strengths and weaknesses, and use your resources to provide the best classroom learning experience for them.

Perception disabilities

Perception disabilities occur when there is an interruption in the input process from the eyes or ears to the neurons in the brain. These disabilities are different than someone who is near- or farsighted, or who has hearing problems. The two main groups of perception disabilities are visual and auditory. Visual perception can be affected in three ways: figure-ground, depth perception or visual-motor. These mainly affect how a child processes information, and may have cause a child to have trouble reading or affect their gross motor skills. These children may have trouble judging the distance between themselves and other objects, and have difficulties with sports that require quick hand-eye coordination. Children with auditory perception difficulties may have trouble determining the differences between sounds in language. Or they may have difficulty hearing a voice in a room with many voices and appear to not be paying attention.

Sensory perception disorder

A sensory perception disorder is one with which any tactile activity can cause discomfort and even pain. Some children are particularly sensitive to touch and this is usually discovered early on, when, as an infant, he will not like being touched or held.

In a classroom, he may be fidgety, complaining of the tag on his shirt or rearranging clothes or his shoes. He will not want to sit too close to anyone in classroom, thus requiring a specific place in any classroom seating place. He may appear to be anti-social because he hovers around the edges of groups, seeming to not want to join in, or be to shy to do so.

Learning disabilities

A learning disability is a disorder of the brain. It occurs when the way the information transmitted in the brain does so a little differently. It does not mean that the brain is damaged, but rather that when the brain was in its earliest stage of development that something affected it. The four main parts of the brain most often affected are language skills, muscle skills, thinking skills and organization skills. A person with difficulty with language may struggle with reading or writing. Someone with a muscle skill disability may have problems with catching a ball or judging depth and distance. A thinking skills disability may affect problem solving or processing information. Many children with an organizational disability have trouble keeping track of their possessions and assignments.

ADD

Signs

Teachers should have little trouble identifying those students who may be suffering from attention deficit disorder, as the behavior of these students will probably be disruptive. Students with ADD usually make careless mistakes in their work and have a hard time sustaining their attention during long lecture periods. They are typically disorganized and are often losing things. They may fidget a great deal with their hands, and just seem to have a great deal of nervous energy. They often talk too much and out of turn. They often have a difficult time working quietly and keeping their hands off of the other students. Many students are so afflicted by attention deficit disorder that they almost seem to be possessed, or driven by some internal motor.

ADHD

Attention deficit hyperactivity disorder (ADHD) is classified by inappropriate amounts of inattention, impulsiveness and hyperactivity. All three behaviors do not need to exist in order for a child to be diagnosed with ADHD. Hyperactivity is usually defined as being fidgety, squirmy or restless on a regular basis. Inattention occurs when they are distracted by both visual and auditory stimuli. They also may daydream and be distracted by other thoughts or ideas easily and have trouble sustaining a conversation. Impulsiveness shows when children seem to be unable to think before they act, therefore they have trouble learning from previous experiences and will tend to repeat undesirable behavior such as calling out, or becoming physical and grabbing a pencil or hitting another child.

Diagnosis and treatment

There are many symptoms of ADHD that are common with children and adolescents and therefore it can be difficult to make an accurate diagnosis since there is not one fool-proof way of assessing ADHD. Usually, ADHD is declared using five steps, outlined in the DSM-IV-TR. Teachers may be given forms that have certain criteria of behavior on them, and give their point of view on the behavior seen over the past six months. This is usually compared with the clinical and family histories, after which a diagnosis can be made. Treatments for ADHD include both medication and non-medication methods. There are a wide variety of drugs for the treatment of ADHD, and the level of success depends on the individual child. Non-medication treatment could include therapy and small group help at school once the school is aware of the diagnosis.

Intellectual disabilities

Intellectual disability is a term that is used to describe people who have abnormal limitations on their levels of mental functioning. These could be in communicating, taking care of themselves and social skills. Due to these limitations, their development has been altered and they will develop at a slower rate than most children. Learning to speak and walk, as well as dressing themselves and eating will take longer to acquire. They are still able to learn, but often require more time and more assistance in order for this to take place. There may be things, such as abstract concepts, that they will never be able to fully comprehend. About 10% the students receiving special education in schools have some form of intellectual disabilities.

The four main causes of intellectual disabilities are:
- Perinatal problems: These are problems that occur during labor and birth, such as the baby not receiving enough oxygen when it is born.
- Problems during pregnancy: Intellectual disabilities can occur when the conditions in the womb are altered in some way when the baby is developing. For example, if a woman drinks or uses drugs during pregnancy, or gets a serious infection.
- Genetic conditions: This occurs when both parents have abnormalities in their genes; for example, Down syndrome is a genetic condition.
- Health problems: Exposure to certain diseases such as the measles or meningitis can cause intellectual disabilities. Also, extreme malnutrition or exposure to poisons, such as arsenic or mercury can also cause problems.

The diagnosis can be made by looking at two main things: the ability of a person's brain to learn, think, problem-solve, or make sense of their surroundings, and whether the person has the skills he needs in order to live independently. The first one—intellectual functioning—can be measured by an IQ test. The average score is 100 and people who score below 75 on the test are considered to have intellectual disabilities. To measure the second one, or their adaptive behavior, observations are done in social environments to see how the person reacts compared to others his age, such as going to the bathroom and feeding himself, as well as interacting and communicating with others.

Behavioral disorders

Students who have emotional and behavioral disturbances exhibit significant behavioral excesses or deficits. Many labels are used to denote deviant behavior; these labels include: emotionally handicapped or disturbed, behaviorally disordered, socially maladjusted, delinquent, mentally ill, psychotic, and schizophrenic. Each of these terms refers to patterns of behavior that depart significantly from the expectations of others. In recent years, "behavioral disorders" has gained favor over "emotional disturbance" as a more accurate label leading to more objective decision-making and fewer negative connotations.

Patterns of disordered behavior

There is considerable agreement about general patterns or types of disordered behavior. One researcher suggests two discrete patterns that he calls "externalizers" (aggressive, disruptive, acting out) and "internalizers" (withdrawn, anxious, depressed). He identifies the following four dimensions:
- Conduct disorders (aggression, disobedience, irritability)
- Personality Disorders (withdrawal, anxiety, physical complaints)
- Immaturity (passivity, poor coping, preference for younger playmates)
- Socialized delinquency (involvement in gang subcultures).

In addition to these, other researchers discuss pervasive developmental disorders (including autism and childhood schizophrenia) and learning disorders (including attention deficit disorders with hyperactivity). Not all behaviorally disordered students experience academic difficulties, but the two factors are often associated.

SED

IDEA defines a serious emotional disturbance (SED) as "a condition exhibiting one or more of the following characteristics over a long period of time and to a marked degree, which adversely affects educational performance:
- An inability to learn which cannot be explained by intellectual, sensory, or health factors.
- An inability to build or maintain satisfactory interpersonal relationships with peers and teachers.

- Inappropriate types of behavior or feelings under normal circumstances.
- A general pervasive mood of unhappiness or depression.
- A tendency to develop physical symptoms or fears associated with personal or school problems." The federal definition includes children who are diagnosed as schizophrenic, but excludes socially maladjusted children "unless it is determined that they are seriously emotionally disturbed." Although autism was formerly included under the SED designation, in 1981 it was transferred to the category of "other health impaired."

ODD

Oppositional Defiant Disorder (ODD) is less common than ADHD or ADD, but is still classified as a behavioral disorder that some children will have. It is classified as consisting of behavior that is negative, defiant, disobedient and hostile toward figures of authority, such as parents, teachers or other adults, but must last for at least six months. Most behavioral disorders need to be observed for at least this period of time before they can be correctly diagnosed. The most typical ways in which an ODD manifests itself are arguing with authority figures, refusing to follow requests or directions, deliberately annoying people by becoming inappropriate, and blaming others for their actions. They do not usually include aggression towards animals or people, or actions of a destructive nature, such as vandalism or theft.

CD

Students who are diagnosed with a Conduct Disorder (CD) usually exhibit certain behaviors that are associated with a CD. These behaviors include an early onset of sexual behavior, smoking and drinking, as well as unnecessary risk taking. It is defined as a pattern of behavior that violates the basic rights of others, or significant social norms and rules specific to their age group. They often stay out late, run away from home, or skip school. They may physically harm other children or animals and due to this may not have many positive social interactions because they always are doing things according to their rules with little regard for others' feelings or property.

Prevalence of emotional and behavioral disturbance

Estimates of the number of school-age children and adolescents with emotional or behavioral disorders depend on the definitions and criteria that are used. At some point in their lives, most individuals exhibit behavior that others consider excessive or inappropriate for the circumstances. Thus, frequency, intensity, duration, and context must be considered in making judgments of disturbance. Unlike some other educational disabilities, emotional and behavioral disorders are not necessarily lifelong conditions. Although teachers typically consider 10–20 percent of their students as having emotional or behavioral problems, a conservative estimate of the number whose problems are both severe and chronic is 2-3 percent of the school-age population. Currently, less than one-half that number are formally identified and receive special education services.

Gifted Children

Former U. S. Commissioner of Education Sidney P. Marland, Jr., in his August 1971 report to Congress, stated, "Gifted and talented children are those identified by professionally qualified persons who by virtue of outstanding abilities are capable of high performance. These are children who require differentiated educational programs and/or services beyond those normally provided by the regular school program in order to realize their contribution to self and society". The same report continued: "Children capable of high performance include those with demonstrated achievement and/or potential ability in any of the following areas, singly or in combination:
- general intellectual ability
- specific academic aptitude
- creative or productive thinking
- leadership ability
- visual or performing arts
- psychomotor ability.

The following are some general characteristics of a gifted student (These are typical factors stressed by educational authorities as being indicative of giftedness. Obviously, no child is outstanding in all characteristics.):
- Shows superior reasoning powers and marked ability to handle ideas; can generalize readily from specific facts and can see subtle relationships; has outstanding problem-solving ability.
- Shows persistent intellectual curiosity; asks searching questions; shows exceptional interest in the nature of man and the universe.
- Has a wide range of interests, often of an intellectual kind
- Is markedly superior in quality and quantity of written or spoken vocabulary; is interested in the subtleties of words and their uses.
- Reads avidly and absorbs books well beyond his or her years.
- Learns quickly and easily and retains what is learned; recalls important details, concepts and principles; comprehends readily.
- Shows insight into arithmetical problems that require careful reasoning and grasps mathematical concepts readily.

- 11 -

- Shows creative ability or imaginative expression in such things as music, art, dance, drama; shows finesse in bodily control.
- Sustains concentration for lengthy periods and shows outstanding responsibility and independence in classroom work.
- Sets realistically high standards for self; is self-critical in evaluation. Shows initiative and originality in intellectual work; shows flexibility in thinking and considers problems from a number of viewpoints.
- Observes keenly and is responsive to new ideas.
- Shows social poise and a mature ability to communicate with adults.
- Gets excitement and pleasure from intellectual challenge; shows an alert and subtle sense of humor.

TAG students can be the most challenging types of students that teachers have in their classroom. Students who are gifted are extremely bright and grasp ideas readily, and even apply their own interpretations to ideas you present of which you might not even be aware. Their level of creativity is displayed in their original thinking and creations. They do have special needs, however, and can be overlooked in the classroom because they seem to be self-sufficient in acquiring the new material, but do require consideration because of their level of intelligence. Most people are slow to realize that gifted children do require special adaptations. When gifted students are not assisted, many become dropouts or feel understimulated in school and as a result, most of our brightest and most talented students become turned off or underdeveloped.

Inclusion
Research indicates that the needs of students who are gifted can be met in the inclusive classroom under certain prerequisite conditions; for example, (1) the students are appropriately grouped in clusters or other homogeneous arrangement; (2) teachers match their instructional strategies to the specific learning needs of the students; (3) the students receive an appropriately differentiated curriculum or have access to the full range of curriculum. Access to the full range of curriculum may be achieved in many ways; for example, through distance education programs, acceleration, or specially designed programs. It is not easy for teachers to provide a learning environment where each child is working at his or her level of challenge, particularly in an inclusive classroom. However, homogeneous or cluster grouping makes it easier for teachers to differentiate curriculum and use strategies such as curriculum compacting that have proven to be effective. Additional strategies for providing effective differentiated instruction are discussed in the literature included in this frequently asked question.

Dual exceptionalities

Gifted students with disabling conditions remain a major group of underserved and under-stimulated youth. The focus on accommodations for their disabilities may preclude the recognition and development of their cognitive abilities. It is not unexpected, then, to find a significant discrepancy between the measured academic potential of these students and their actual performance in the classroom. In order for these children to reach their potential, it is imperative that their intellectual strengths be recognized and nurtured, at the same time as their disability is accommodated appropriately.

Assessment
Identification of giftedness in students who are disabled is problematic. The customary identification methods (i.e., standardized tests and observational checklists) are inadequate without major modification. Standard lists of characteristics of gifted

students may be inadequate for unmasking hidden potential in children who have disabilities. Children whose hearing is impaired, for example, cannot respond to oral directions, and they may also lack the vocabulary which reflects the complexity of their thoughts. Children whose speech or language is impaired cannot respond to tests requiring verbal responses. Children whose vision is impaired may be unable to respond to certain performance measures, and although their vocabulary may be quite advanced, they may not understand the full meaning of the words they use (e.g., color words). Children with learning disabilities may use high-level vocabulary in speaking but be unable to express themselves in writing, or vice versa. In addition, limited life experiences due to impaired mobility may artificially lower scores. Because the population of gifted/disabled students is difficult to locate, they are seldom included in standardized test norming groups, adding to the problems of comparison. In addition, gifted children with disabilities often use their intelligence to try to circumvent the disability. This may cause both exceptionalities to appear less extreme; using one to mask the other normalizes both.

ADA

The Americans with Disabilities Act (ADA) was passed by Congress in 1990. This act outlines the rights of individuals with disabilities in society in all ways besides education. It states that they should receive nondiscriminatory treatment in jobs, access to businesses and other stores, as well as other services. Due to this law, all businesses must be wheelchair accessible, having a ramp that fits the standards of the law, and making sure that all doors are wide enough and that bathrooms can be maneuvered by someone in a wheelchair. If these rules are not followed, businesses can be subject to large fines until these modifications have been complied with. The ADA also ensures fair treatment when applying for jobs to make sure that there is no unfair discrimination for any person with a disability who is applying to the job.

IDEA

The Individuals with Disabilities Education Act (IDEA) is the law that guarantees all children with disabilities access to a free and appropriate public education. It addresses the educational needs of children from birth through age 21 and accounts for 13 categories of educational special needs. IDEA amended the public law passed in 1975, which was known as the Education for All Handicapped Children Act, or PL 94-142. This law ensures that all students with disabilities receive an education that is appropriate to them. The definition that IDEA gives to children with disabilities can include speech or language impairments, autism, brain injury, hearing impairment, learning disabilities and intellectual disabilities. Children from birth to school age also have access to certain state resources, if their state participates in supplying such services. This may include speech and language pathology or family counseling depending on their needs. A written IEP is outlined for each child once they reach school age, and the main stipulation that it makes is that each child should be educated in the least restrictive environment, which may mean a regular classroom setting for the child.

Mainstreaming and inclusion

Traditional mainstreaming in public schools is defined as allowing students with physical disabilities to be placed in certain regular education classes. As practiced in the 1970s and early '80s, mainstreaming was an attempt to meet the LRE requirement by moving students from separate schools and classes into regular education classes for part or all of the school day. Often, students received their academic instruction in special classes and their time with nondisabled peers was

- 13 -

spent in nonacademic activities such as lunch, recess, physical education, or perhaps art and music. This seems to be an easy thing to do, but the fact is that in order for this to be effective and beneficial for all the students involved, there must be the correct support services in place. Otherwise, the classroom teacher may be spread too thin if she is expected to differentiate for the student with the disability on her own. Due to this some schools will only mainstream children with mild to moderate disabilities, instead of all students with disabilities. If a school is fully committed to the idea of mainstreaming students with disabilities, it should be done so with support in the regular classroom in order to make the transition run smoothly.

Mainstreaming, when done correctly, can have many positive effects on social performance. If the students in the regular classroom are educated about the students with disabilities that could be entering their classrooms, then the rate of success tends to be much higher. If no transition work is done, then isolation can be the result, which is the exact opposite of the goal of mainstreaming. For academic performance, as long as the right support systems are in place in the regular classroom (such as a paraeducator and any necessary adaptations to the assigned work), then the academic performance of students with disabilities can only improve. Mainstreaming is meant to increase awareness and to welcome diversity, and when done properly, a classroom is a great place in which for this change to occur.

The traditional idea of mainstreaming allows students with disabilities to participate in some regular classrooms whereas inclusion allows these same students the ability to participate in all regular classrooms and activities. Generally, inclusion is thought of as the better option to better avoid the segregation that can sometime occur between students with disabilities and

without. If they are mainstreamed, they are only mainstreamed in certain classes, whereas with inclusion, more possibilities are open to them, and depending on what is outlined in their IEP, they may have one-on-one support in the classrooms they are in. It also gives them the opportunity to participate in the same activities that all students participate in to the greatest extent possible, thus following the order that all students with disabilities be educated in the least restrictive environment possible.

Inclusion is the meaningful participation of students with disabilities in general education classrooms. To practice inclusion successfully the school principal and staff must understand the history, terms, and legal requirements involved as well as have the necessary levels of support and commitment. The word inclusion is not a precise term, and it is often confused with similar concepts such as least restrictive environment (LRE) and mainstreaming. Educating children in the least restrictive environment has been mandated since the 1970s, when it was a major provision of the Education for All Handicapped Children Act. The law states that to the maximum extent appropriate, children with disabilities are educated with children who are nondisabled; and that special classes, separate schooling, or other removal of children from the regular educational environment occurs only if the nature or severity of the disability is such that education in regular classes with the use of supplemental aids and services cannot be achieved satisfactorily.

Pros and cons of inclusion

Inclusion is defined as the commitment to educate the child, to the highest possible effect, in a regular school and classroom. It outlines bringing the support to the students in the classroom, such as special supplies, or other teachers, rather than separating them in separate rooms or buildings altogether. People who support inclusion could argue that students with disabilities who are educated separately are being discriminated against and therefore it violates their rights. They also voice a need for reform in the special education programs, which they argue are costly for the often inadequate results that they produce, both academically and socially. However, some special educators and teachers have voiced their concerns that inclusion could result in insufficient services for students with disabilities. A regular classroom may not be the place for children with behavioral problems or anti-social disorders. There is also the concern that inclusion could replace special education altogether one day.

Least restrictive environment

IDEA sets out goals for how to achieve an equal education for students with disabilities. One part of it is that students with disabilities are educated in the least restrictive environment, the goal of which is to be educated in a regular classroom. They should be able to participate in regular education programs to the greatest extent allowed. Segregating students with disabilities can be detrimental to their social development, and IDEA feels that educating them is beneficial to all students instead of hiding them away in other classrooms or buildings. Even though social benefits can be strong, they must be based against individual circumstances and the best environment in which a student can be educated can only be judged on a case-by-case basis.

Oberti test

Court cases have produced guidelines that can be helpful in determining the best placement for a student. One of these is Oberti v. Board of Education, which specified three considerations for determining placement: (1) the steps taken by the school to try to include the child in the general education classroom; (2) the comparison between the educational benefit the child would receive in a general education classroom, including social and communication benefits, and the benefits the child would receive in a segregated classroom, and (3) possible negative effects inclusion would have on the other children in the general education class.

Physical education for disabled students

Adapted physical education is an individualized program of developmental activities, exercises, games, rhythms and sports designed to meet the unique physical education needs of individuals with disabilities. Adapted physical education may take place in classes that range from those in regular physical education (i.e., students who are mainstreamed) to those in self contained classrooms. Although an adapted physical education program is individualized, it can be implemented in a group setting. It should be geared to each student's needs, limitations, and abilities. Whenever appropriate, students receiving an adapted physical education program should be included in regular physical education settings. Adapted physical education is an active program of physical activity rather than a sedentary alternative program. It supports the attainment of the benefits of physical activity by meeting the needs of students who might otherwise be relegated to passive experiences associated with physical education. In establishing adapted physical education programs, educators work with parents, students, teachers, administrators, and professionals in various disciplines. Adapted physical education may employ developmental, community-based, or other orientations and may use a variety of teaching styles. It takes place in schools and other agencies responsible for educating individuals.

IEP

IDEA sets out the steps to ensure that each student with a disability has access to a fair and equal education. One component of this is that each student diagnosed with a disability should have an Individualized Education Program (IEP), which is a written statement made in conjunction with the student, parents/guardians, school officials and teachers. It must include an analysis of the student's present achievement level, outline goals, both long-term and short term, as well as describe the steps to be taken to assist the student in achieving these goals. It should also specify the extent to which the student will be able to participate in regular education programs. It should be clear about the length and duration of these services and gives the details of how this program will be checked for any necessary revisions and the progress achieved.

Special education teachers help to develop an Individualized Education Program (IEP) for each special education student. The IEP sets personalized goals for each student and is tailored to the student's individual needs and ability. When appropriate, the program includes a transition plan outlining specific steps to prepare students with disabilities for middle school or high school or, in the case of older students, a job or postsecondary study. Teachers review the IEP with the student's parents, school administrators, and the student's general education teacher. Teachers work closely with parents to inform them of their child's progress and suggest techniques to promote learning at home.

In the creation of an IEP, there can be disputes as to what is best for each student, and due process protects the rights of parents to have their voices heard in this process. If parents and school officials disagree with one another, an impartial hearing may take place for mediation, where both sides meet with an impartial person who helps them find terms upon which both can agree upon. There also may be an impartial due process hearing between both parties who present their

cases and a hearing officer decides what is appropriate based on the law requirements. All parents should receive an outline of special education procedures which describes the steps for due process hearings and mediation.

Section 504 of the Rehabilitation Act

Section 504 of the Rehabilitation Act (regarding nondiscrimination under federal grants and programs) states:
Sec. 504.(a) No otherwise qualified individual with a disability in the United States, as defined in section 7(20), shall, solely by reason of her or his disability, be excluded from the participation in, be denied the benefits of, or be subjected to discrimination under any program or activity receiving Federal financial assistance or under any program or activity conducted by any Executive agency or by the United States Postal Service. The head of each such agency shall promulgate such regulations as may be necessary to carry out the amendments to this section made by the Rehabilitation, Comprehensive Services, and Developmental Disabilities Act of 1978.

Section 504 protects qualified individuals with disabilities. Under this law, individuals with disabilities are defined as persons with a physical or mental impairment which substantially limits one or more major life activities. People who have a history of, or who are regarded as having a physical or mental impairment that substantially limits one or more major life activities, are also covered. Major life activities include caring for one's self, walking, seeing, hearing, speaking, breathing, working, performing manual tasks, and learning. In addition to meeting the above definition, for purposes of receiving services, education or training, qualified individuals with disabilities are persons who meet normal and essential eligibility requirements. For purposes of employment, qualified individuals with disabilities are persons who, with

- 16 -

reasonable accommodation, can perform the essential functions of the job for which they have applied or have been hired to perform. (Complaints alleging employment discrimination on the basis of disability against a single individual will be referred to the U. S. Equal Employment Opportunity Commission for processing.) Reasonable accommodation means an employer is required to take reasonable steps to accommodate your disability unless it would cause the employer undue hardship.

Section 504 was enacted to "level the playing field"; to eliminate impediments to full participation by persons with disabilities. In legal terms, the statute was intended to prevent intentional or unintentional discrimination against persons with disabilities, persons who are believed to have disabilities, or family members of persons with disabilities. Though enacted almost 25 years ago, until recently Section 504 has been largely ignored by schools. Given the statute's tempestuous history, this is little short of shocking. Two years after Section 504 was enacted, advocates held highly publicized demonstrations on the doorstep of the then-U.S. Department of Health, Education and Welfare simply to get the Department to adopt implementing regulations. But since then, the statute, regulations and their mandate have been considered by many as the "black hole" of the education law universe.

The most important issues in Section 504 of the Rehabilitation Services Act are as follows:

- People with disabilities have the same rights and must receive the same benefits as people without disabilities when they are applying for jobs or when they are employees.
- All medical services and instruction available to the public must be available to people with disabilities.

- They are entitled to participation in any vocational assistance, day care or any other government program on an equal basis as those who do not have disabilities.
- Selection to college, job-training or post-high school education programs must be based on academic records, not by disability. For example, someone with a learning disability can take a modified version of the ACT entrance exam.
- An appropriate elementary and secondary education must be provided for all students with disabilities.

Differences from IDEA
There are a number of differences between the two statutes, which have very different, but complementary, objectives. Perhaps the most important is, as has been stated, that Section 504 is intended to establish a "level playing field" (usually by eliminating barriers that exclude persons with disabilities) whereas IDEA is remedial (often requiring the provision of programs and services in addition to those available to persons without disabilities). Thus, Section 504 precludes hurdles to participation, whether physical (e.g., steps that prevent a person in a wheelchair from accessing a building) or programmatic (e.g., excluding a child with hepatitis from a classroom). By distinction, IDEA is similar to an "affirmative action" law: as some have asserted, school children with disabilities who fall within IDEA's coverage are sometimes granted "more" services or additional protections than children without disabilities. The "more" and "additional" denote another important difference between Section 504 and IDEA. While IDEA requires "more" of schools for children of disabilities, it also provides schools with additional, if insignificant, funding. Section 504 requires that schools not discriminate, and in some cases

undertake actions that require additional expenditures, but provides no additional financial support. For this reason, schools often drag their feet in providing needed services to children under Section 504, and are less hesitant to openly discuss the limitations of funding.

Relationship to the ADA
The Americans With Disabilities Act (ADA), enacted in 1990, has deep roots in Section 504. In many ways, the ADA is Section 504 "writ large." The primary difference is that while Section 504 applies only to organizations that receive Federal funding, the ADA applies to a much broader universe. However, with respect to education, the ADA's objectives and language are very similar to Section 504, and for this reason both statutes are administered by the Office for Civil Rights and considered essentially identical.

Family involvement in special education services

As IDEA has been amended, each time more care has been given to the role of families in special education. There are several levels of parental rights given for the level of special education that their children receive from birth through age 21. This could be consent, participation in the educational decisions about their children, policy making and notification. Parental involvement for infants and toddlers with disabilities is especially strong due to the availability of services for the entire family.

Differentiating task content

Differentiating the content requires that students are pre-tested in some degree so that the teacher can tell which students do not require direct instruction and instead can do some independently guided learning. This would occur if perhaps some students already understand the concept and can begin applying the concept to solve a problem. Another way of doing this is

simply to have able students accelerate their rate of progress by outlining their own course of action for the task. This will allow the teacher enough time to go over the content of a task in enough detail that other students will be able to understand it thoroughly before moving on to the next step.

Differentiating task process

To have differentiation in the process of a task means that students need a variety of learning activities and strategies in order to be able to explore the concepts in the best way possible. They need to be made aware of all the possible ways to manipulate and consider the ideas in the concept. Some ways of assisting this would be graphic organizers, charts, graphs or diagrams in order to display their understanding of the material covered. By varying the required complexity of the graphic organizer, this allows for each student to be challenged according to their ability. This would work well in a classroom with a wide variety of students because it is most independently guided work.

Differentiating the final product

By having a variety of products that the students can produce, they will be more likely to choose something that catches their interest, therefore having some intrinsic motivation to do well at the task. The product can be varied in complexity depending upon what ability level upon which each student is working. Students who are working below grade level may have the performance expectations reduced, whereas students who are working above grade level may be asked to demonstrate higher and more complex learning processes in their adaptation of the product. By giving the students the choice of what they are working on, a natural differentiation occurs because each student will automatically adjust the task to his ability level.

Second language acquisition

The first two steps that occur in second language acquisition are:

- Stage 1: Pre-production: Most English language learners (ELL) will have a limited range of English words but will not speak voluntarily. They may repeat what you say to them, and be able to copy from the board. Observing body language is important at this stage in order to judge the student's progress when it cannot be done through language.
- Stage 2: Early production: This stage will last for about six months in which the student will learn to speak in one or two word phrases. They can use memorized sentences although they might not be used correctly. Assigning a language buddy at these two stages will be helpful. Remember, however, that for these students, it is exhaustive to be attempting to learn a new language for an entire school day, so progress may be slow to appear.

Helping ELL students

It may be helpful to introduce aspects of the English Language Learner (ELL) student's culture and language to the other students in order to have a smooth transition. Then other students may approach the ELL student in order for them to build up confidence talking to peers, which will often happen before they feel comfortable talking to adults. It is also helpful to ask clear cut "yes or no" questions and not expect more than "yes or no" answers. Depending on the language, having a dictionary of their language in the classroom may be helpful if the student does not bring one themselves. The student should have the chance to participate in whole class activities. Using pictures to increase vocabulary is also an effective way to convey ideas to ELL students and can help their spelling and reading skills as well.

Multicultural education

Multicultural education is education that sees to enrich each student's perspective by valuing pluralism and studying a variety of cultures. It seeks to lessen prejudices and increase tolerance, and ensure that minority students are receiving a fair and equal education. It does not believe in the analogy of the melting pot, where all cultures blend together, but celebrates the differences and aims instead for a "mixed salad" where individual cultures are distinct from each other, but form a unique whole as they are put together. It accepts and praises the differences in the individual and tries to project that there is not a typical American, but that everyone who lives here is American.

Criticisms
Some criticisms of multicultural education are concerned about the potential damage that pluralism could have on schools. They fear that many common traditions, values and purposes may be eradicated because of the focus on other cultures and traditions. The main idea that some critics would have is that multicultural education teaches that everything is of equal value and that the schools have a responsibility to teach about all of these values. It is also judged as a reform movement against the discrimination of students who are discriminated against because of their language, race, religion, sex, or age.

Multicultural backgrounds

Nonwhite students now comprise 1/3 of the under-18 population in the US. The recent growth is especially large in Latino and Asian populations; two populations which within themselves are extremely diverse. This will cause continued growth in the number of students who enter school who are ELL and whose family backgrounds may not correlate with the norms and expectations schools may have. Many of these children will succeed in school and adapt successfully to the school culture. If ELL students do not acquire English to a satisfactory level, their language barrier may cause them to have low levels of achievement and eventually even cause them to drop out of school altogether. Having family support is important for any student to succeed in school, but if the parents do not speak English at all, then it can be difficult for their children to succeed as well.

Bilingual education

There are three main types of bilingual education: the submersion model, where the students are dropped into all-English classes and must learn English or fail; the immersion model, where students are taught by a teacher who understands their language but only speaks in English to them; and the transitional model, where the child's native tongue is used only to transition and explain English to them until they achieve fluency. Other lesser used types of bilingual education include maintenance and ESL, where there is a mix of instruction in the native language, and teachers who do not know their native language who teach the basics of the English language until fluency is enough to attend regular English classes more often.

Controversy
With an influx of Spanish speakers, many states have hurried English-only legislation that makes English the official language of the state. Some groups assert that bilingual education actually impedes the English skills of minorities since they are receiving their education primarily in their native language. Some would also argue that English is the language of the U.S. and that students should study the language of the country in which they live. However, there are many benefits to bilingual education, and many studies have proven that children

who have the knowledge of two or more languages tend to achieve higher academically than those students who only know their native language. Certain bilingual programs have proven to be more effective than others, such as immersion programs or programs gradually including English instruction over a period of time.

Lau vs. Nichols case
English as a Second Language students (ESL) comprise one of the most hidden failure groups in American schools. Due to their difficulty in understanding, speaking and writing English, they fall further behind in school and increasing numbers drop out altogether. In 1974, a group of Chinese speaking children had a class action suit filed on their behalf in San Francisco. The San Francisco school system allegedly discriminated against the students by not helping with their language problems. The Lau case did not make bilingual education mandatory, but it paved the way for other states to start bilingual programs. The U.S. Office of Civil Rights outlined the Lau Remedies, or ways in which bilingual programs could be instigated, mainly that students should be taught in their native language until they could benefit from receiving instruction on the English language.

Cultural and social development

Culture provides the medium from which most children acquire their knowledge. Also, culture gives children a chance to put their knowledge into experience. Therefore, culture can teach children both what and how to think. Children learn most of their experiences through interaction with someone else, namely parents or teachers, but sometimes siblings and peers. Eventually, children assume the responsibility of solving problems for themselves and not relying on others for help. Language is the main way in which these transactions take place and therefore language is important in both the social and cultural development, because through it are conveyed many hidden messages about what is acceptable both culturally and socially; for example, swearing is not allowed in a school culture, but may be viewed highly in a social setting of other children. It is mainly through personal experience that the differences are determined for each child.

School culture

The culture of a school is defined as the set of norms, values, beliefs, symbols and rituals that make up the school. These are built up over time as the parents, teachers, parents and students work together in order to solve problems. Schools also have rituals that take place in order to build up a sense of school community, such as assemblies, plays, or sporting events. It can also be conveyed by the atmosphere of the school and the appearance of the staff and students. How the staff functions together and with the administrators is also important to see whether it is positive or negative. If student groups are able to meet readily with teachers and administrators and be able to collaborate in problem solving, then this usually provides a good pathway in order to have a positive environment between the students and the adults in the building.

Social and emotional issues

Adolescence is a roller coaster of a time, and these difficulties often manifest themselves in various ways in the classroom. Sexism, racism, and homophobia will often appear in many ways as the students are going through puberty and are enjoying the novelty of these issues. It is important to maintain a safe environment in any classroom, therefore these sorts of comments should not be tolerated, a fact which should be made clear from the start. Students could be dealing with any one of these issues in

their home life as some parents perceive their getting older as needing more responsibilities at home. Some students will also become more rebellious and try drugs, smoking or drinking. Maintaining a mature attitude towards these topics and trying to integrate them into the curriculum is beneficial as it will provide real-life experience to the students going through any problems.

Motivation and associated misconceptions

Motivation is defined as the selection, direction and continuation of behavior. Some teachers believe that some students are unmotivated, which is not a correct statement. As long as each student is able to set goals for himself and able to achieve them, then he will not be unmotivated. What is usually meant by this is that students are not motivated to behave in the way teachers would like them to behave. Another misconception is that one person, usually a teacher, can directly motivate another person or a student. This is also inaccurate because motivation comes from within the student. Teachers need to be able to use all kinds of motivation theories in their classroom in order to be able to find that which motivates all of their students. The more ideas students are exposed to, the easier this will be able to happen.

Cognitive view of motivation

The cognitive view of motivation believes that behavior is influenced by the way that people think about themselves and the environment in which they are. There are four influences that explain how the direction of this behavior takes place. The first is the intrinsic need to have a logically constructed knowledge base, which means that people need to make sense of their experiences. Knowing what one's expectations are for completing a task successfully is the second influence, because there needs to be a certain amount of self-awareness in order to react positively to an occurrence and repeat the experience. The third influence are the factors that one believes account for success and failure, such as education and perseverance, and the fourth is one's belief about his own ability to solve problems and think critically.

Control theory

The control theory describes how our motivations, behaviors and actions are attempts to satisfy needs such as love, survival, power and freedom. If we are able to understand these needs and how we try to pursue them, then we can choose on how best to meet them. When teachers use this intrinsic motivation with their students, the result can be that students see how they feel when work is completed, and strive to always improve themselves. Many students express that their favorite part of going to school is being with their friends (a built-in need) and therefore group work, or cooperative learning, can satisfy this need instead of independent seatwork or teacher lectures. Cooperative learning can end inappropriate behaviors that are seeking power, and instead work of the concept that in small groups, students will be listening to each other, which will in turn foster a sense of self-respect and importance.

B.F. Skinner

Reinforcement
Reinforcement explains that behavior is a function of its consequences, meaning that a student will repeat a certain behavior, such as raising his hand to answer a question if the consequences are desirable, such as positive reinforcement from the teacher about his answer. This could be either a verbal response, such as "That was a great answer," or points that lead to extra credit or a tangible reward. It is important that the reward is something that is of interest to the student in order for this model to be effective. On the other hand, if an

inappropriate behavior, such as calling out, is given a positive reinforcement, such as attention from the teacher, instead of the teacher ignoring the student, ideally leading to extinction of the behavior, then the student will continue the undesirable behavior. Criticism of this theory includes that it is too rigid and quantifies human behavior instead of qualifying it.

Operant conditioning
Studying his operant conditioning interpretations of learning may help teachers learn why some students react positively to certain subjects and why they will dislike others. Some students will enter a certain class, like art, with excitement and ready to learn, whereas some will enter the classroom reluctantly. This is due to past experiences. The student who loves art may have had positive experiences with previous art teachers, and another student may not have. Skinner would argue that the student who loves art is that way because of a number of positive experiences that have reinforced that love of art. A student who does not like art feels that way because of a series of negative experiences, not necessarily because he is poor at the subject.

FAPE

FAPE (Free Appropriate Public Education) is requirement coined in order to comply with the federal mandate, Public Law 102-119, known as the Individuals with Disabilities Education Act. More specifically, part B of the act, which mandated that all disabled children receive a free appropriate public education and as such a school district must provide special education and related services at no cost to the child or his parents.

Planning and Delivering Instruction and Education Technology

Experiential learning

Kolb outlined four stages that occur when learning is taking place. It begins at any stage and is continuous, meaning that there is no limit to the number of times each stage is experienced. These stages define learning as occurring through concrete experience, observation and reflection, abstract conceptualization, or active experimentation. As we have more experience at being learners, we tend to start at the same stage for all of our learning processes. For example, a student might come up with an idea for a science fair project (abstract conceptualization), and then proceed to experiment with different ways of presenting the information (active experimentation), then create the final product (concrete experience) and write up the report to accompany the project (observation and reflection). Depending on each person's learning style, they may start at a different stage every time, or stick with the one that works best for them after repeated successes.

Action learning

Reg Revans' theory of Action Learning is an approach that uses small cooperative learning groups. These groups meet regularly with each other to discuss real-life issues. The aim of these groups is to learn from one another and with each other through the experiences that they share. He believed that action and learning must coincide for the other to exist. By having small groups, possibly ones that students choose in order to feel comfortable, they can develop a rapport and a safe environment in order for these learning sessions to take place. He believed that these groups were successful in finding solutions for problems that do not necessarily have a right or wrong answer, but can benefit from having other individuals and their subjective experiences with whom to discuss a problem.

Constructivism and behaviorism

Constructivism is based on the understanding that due to all of our experiences we construct our own comprehension of the world we live in. We each all create our own mental rules and values to make sense of the experiences we have. Therefore, learning is simply how we adjust our "rules" to include new experiences, which may in turn cause us to reassess our mental rules.

With behaviorism learning is defined as simply the new behavior that we acquire through experiences. It focuses mainly on observable behaviors, such as social interactions or physical exertions, not mental activities or thought processes. These two things are not the focus because they cannot be quantified and therefore cannot be measured in the same ways that observable behavior can.

Piaget's and Vygotsky's learning theories

Piaget created a model of child development and learning that shows how their cognitive structure develops. It is based around the main idea that children build cognitive structures or concepts in order to respond to experiences in their environment. It also becomes more complex as it develops, explaining how children move from simple movements, such as sucking their thumb, to complex mental activities such as reading as they become older.

Vygotsky thought that culture is the main influencing factor on human development and thus created the social cognition learning model. Because humans are the only species to have created culture, every child develops within this context. This culture that influences the development of the child starts with the family environment, but then spreads to the media, school and community.

Piaget's four developmental stages for children are:

- Sensorimotor (birth to 2 years of age): Children build their set of concepts through physical interaction with their environment. They do not have the sense of object permanence that whereas to them it appears that the toy train ceases to exist when it is out of their sight, the toy train still exists.
- Preoperational stage (ages 2-7): They still operate better in concrete situations. Although they may recognize abstract concepts, they are still unable to fully grasp them and their existence.
- Concrete operations (ages 7-11): With more physical experiences, they can start to conceptualize, and may be able to solve abstract problems, such as using numbers in math instead of adding and subtracting physical objects.
- Formal Operations (begins at 11-15): At this stage, children's cognitive structures are like those of an adult and include conceptual reasoning.

Cooperative learning

Classroom tasks can be set so that students are competing with one another, working individually, or cooperating with others in order to receive the awards that teachers make available for completing the work. Usually, competitive arrangements are used, which means that each student is

competing against each other for the best grade. However, cooperative arrangements have an overall better result when students are meant to be working with each other toward a common goal. The benefits of this system tend to be qualitative and may be difficult to measure, because often the real-life experiences students gain by working with each other outweighs all other benefits in the long run.

Sensory stimulation theory

When the senses are stimulated, effective learning can take place. That is the basic definition of sensory stimulation theory. The most effective medium of learning takes place through seeing; this could be by watching a performance of a text done as a play, or watching an experiment conducted by a teacher before the students attempt it themselves. Hearing something is the next most effective way of learning something, and the other senses—smell, taste and touch—all have about the same effectiveness after the others when they are used in learning. The most important part of this theory is that when more than one sense is stimulated—ideally more than two—it is then that the most effective type of learning takes place. This is also along the same lines of multiple intelligences which states that students have more than one type of intelligence that should be used when teaching.

Gestalt approach and holistic learning theory

The Gestalt approach (also known as the cognitive approach) gives experience the most importance in this learning theory because it believes that through active problem-solving insights will develop which are vital to learning because each student approaches each task subjectively and will therefore develop insights that make sense to them individually. The holistic learning theory takes into account that each student has a different personality comprised of many different elements, such as imaginations, feelings and intelligence, that all need to be stimulated if learning is to be achieved.

Humanistic approach to learning

The humanistic approach (facilitation theory) was developed by the work of Carl Rogers and other psychologists. It places the importance of learning upon the person who is facilitating the learning. In order for this to take place, the atmosphere of the classroom needs to be safe in order for new ideas to be explored and risks to be taken. In a classroom that follows the humanistic approach, teachers would be willing to question their own beliefs and values, able to listen to students' experiences, ideas, and especially feelings—as concerned with the relationship with each student as well as what they were teaching—and open to both positive and negative feedback in order to examine their own behavior and teaching style. Students would be given the chance to be responsible for the content of their learning, provide their own experiences and feelings in order to be able to get the most out of what they are learning, learn that self-evaluation is an important part of their learning process and that it provides them the chance to examine their own progress in achieving results or solving problems.

Persuasive Models Social Learning theory

This theory starts with the assertion that individuals will pay attention to positive experiences that they observe and strive to repeat the same experience themselves. This is where consistency is important in a classroom because students will often expect the same response for an observed behavior. This could manifest itself in several ways. A student who admires a teacher of a subject may work hard to please the teacher and to become like them because he sees the teacher as a role model.

Students may strive to achieve high grades like those of their classmates if they overhear them talking about how they get paid for good grades. If a student repeats the same behavior of a previous student but gets a different reward or none at all, the student will continue to be unclear about what the teacher wants from his students.

Prior knowledge

Prior knowledge is a combination of one's attitudes, experiences and knowledge which already exist. Attitudes can range from beliefs about ourselves as learners or being aware of our own strengths and weaknesses. It can also be our level of motivation and responsibility for our own learning. The experiences from our daily activities, especially ones with our friends and families, give us a background from which we derive most of our understanding. Individual events in our lives provide us experiences from which to draw from; both bad and good and influence how we deal with future situations. This knowledge is drawn from a wide variety of things, from knowledge of specific content areas and the concepts within, to the goals that we have for ourselves academically.

It is important that students have accurate and relevant prior knowledge to be used. If prior knowledge is inaccurate, it could negatively affect their performance. A student who has little or no prior knowledge will almost certainly perform better than a student with inaccurate prior knowledge. Accessing prior knowledge can cause awkward situations, especially if students bring up issues that teachers are unable to control and that may be inappropriate and prejudiced. However, using students' prior knowledge can help them to reexamine their current understandings and test their old knowledge with new facts and figures. Prior knowledge must be activated and providing a safe classroom where students feel safe to express their opinions is the first step in having this be successful.

There are several specific methods that teachers can use to activate the prior knowledge of their students. This is important because some students may have valuable prior knowledge but may not be aware of it if it hasn't been activated properly. One way to activate this knowledge is by a word association task. Writing a term on the board at the beginning of a new unit, such as slavery, can be a good way to see what students associate with the term. It is also a beneficial way for the teacher to see what the students already know and plan the unit accordingly. Another way is to use analogies or figures of speech that the students may use without even knowing it. Before introducing a novel, for example, the students could examine the analogy "The straw that broke the camel's back" and then study a novel where that is the main theme.

Preconceptions

Preconceptions are opinions or conceptions formed before adequate knowledge or experience has been accessed. They are often prejudices or biases. Students' preconceptions will often come into the classroom, especially in learner-centered ones. It can only be helpful to integrate these preconceptions into what is studied instead of ignoring them altogether. Firstly, teachers should pay attention to the knowledge that students are bringing into the classroom and be aware of cultural differences. If teachers remain attentive to students' individual progress, then they will be able to fill in the blanks of where the student has gaps in their knowledge due to their preconceptions. It may be useful to provide basic knowledge before a topic is studied and then discuss students' reactions in order to talk about preconceptions and have students recognize that they exist.

Culture

Culture is an aspect of everything that is taught, whether or not teachers are aware of it. The gestures, words and objects used while teaching are all a part of culture. It is important that culture is taught without judgment and that there is not a value placed on one culture over another in the classroom. This is primarily because culture, especially American culture, is not monolithic; cultures require interaction amongst different cultures in order for humans to survive. Similarly, there is a classroom culture that could be much different for most students, and therefore it is important to assess students' preconceptions of classrooms because the rules between each room differ with the teacher.

Critical thinking

Critical thinking is defined as the pursuit of relevant, reasonable and reliable knowledge about the world that is focused on what one should believe or do. Someone who is thinking critically is able to ask appropriate questions, collect information that is relevant, sort through the gathered information, develop reasoning, and come to certain conclusions through this process. Critical thinking is higher order thinking that enables someone to decide on which political candidate to vote for, assess the dangers of gun violence, and many other tasks that are studied in school. Lower-order thinking would be checking to see whether one received the correct change at a grocery store, or being able to tie ones shoes. The goal of critical thinking is to develop responsible citizens who contribute to a healthy, productive society and who don't succumb to its temptations.

Critical thinking is an important skill for all students to learn because it provides students with the tools to be successful and responsible citizens when they have finished school. Due to the fact that children are not born with the power to think critically, and that it is something which

- 26 -

must be taught, in order to successfully educate all students this is a skill that must be aspired to. Since it is a skill that only educated instructors could possess, it is important that adequate time in school is devoted to this task. Students who are able to learn this skill will benefit by being able to question information, being able to think for themselves, challenge traditional beliefs, discover new information and investigate problems.

<u>Controversy</u>

If critical thinking skills enable an individual to think for one's self and make decisions that affect one's life, it could also lead to more rebellion and challenging of authority in schools. If students are taught critical thinking skills, they may learn to not believe just any information given to them and spend all their time questioning everything, instead of it leading to some result, such as becoming more educated. As long as critical thinking is taught with the goal of some end, such as completing a project or experiment, then it is useful to teach this skill in school, and let the students decide whether it is useful to them or not.

A critical thinker:
- Organizes thoughts in order to be able to articulate them,
- Uses evidence relevantly and objectively,
- Only makes a judgment when all evidence has been presented,
- Understands that there are different degrees of belief,
- Sees hidden similarities and analogies,
- Learns independently,
- Applies previous knowledge to new situations to solve problems,
- Can see irrelevancies in verbal arguments and rephrase them concisely,

- Questions ones own views and attempts to assess why those views are held,
- Is sensitive to the difference between intensities and validities of beliefs,
- Is aware that one's knowledge is limited, and
- Recognizes that one's opinions are not always right, that they contain bias, and that there is a danger of including personal preferences in the consideration of evidence.

Creative thinking

Creative thinking is defined as the process by which we derive a new idea. It is the merging of a series of ideas which have not been combined before. New ideas are made when old ones are joined in our minds. Due to the fact that our brains automatically organize information once it is obtained, we can only think about new ideas in the context of what we already know. Therefore, someone who is constantly acquiring new information will have more of a base of information which with to be creative than someone who remains stagnant in their information acquiring process. Creative thinking is something that can be naturally learned, as every day we come into contact with new information that we can use to create new ideas.

Creative thinking can either be accomplished accidentally, deliberately, or by an ongoing process. When creative thinking is done accidentally, it usually is by a chance encounter where one tries something one might not have tried in a different situation. Through this process, progression can take a long time to develop and improve without any guidance. Deliberate creative thinking can be used to create new ideas from a structure. When certain criteria are provided, these techniques can force a wide range of ideas to develop. For example, students may be given a list of five things to include in a story, from which countless stories could emerge. Finally, ongoing creative thinking is a process that develops through education and self-awareness. It is a process by which seeking improvement never ends. For example, a student working on a short story will have to have a sustained level of creative thinking in order to be able to finish the story successfully.

Problem solving

Problem solving is an important skill that is used in all classes. The best way to initiate the cycle of problem solving is to ask questions that will spur students into a dialogue about the problem which will work out how they will begin to attempt the task. If they know what the problem is first, and define everything they know about the task, then they will be better suited to attempt to solve it. If they are able to visualize or imagine the solution, then their experimentation toward the means will have more purpose as they can see what they are working towards. It students are having trouble moving on, or are stuck, encourage them to take a break, by walking around if appropriate, or not looking at the material. Once a solution is found, have the students write down as much as they can in order to avoid other complications that could appear while planning the solution.

There are seven steps that can be used in dealing with any problem that the students will face in a classroom. Introducing this to students can encourage them to use their own resources before they ask for help from the teacher. The first step is to identify the problem. The next is to look for possible causes for the problem. Thirdly, coming up with as many ideas as possible for solving the problem leads to the fourth step which is deciding which is the best way to deal with it. Following this, come up with an action plan just in case the solution doesn't work, which you will then do as you are monitoring how the problem solving is going. The last step is to finalize how the

problem has been solved and if it has done so clearly.

Higher order thinking skills

Bloom's Taxonomy

When developing higher order thinking skills, it is important to use the lower order thinking skills as building blocks. The lower thinking skills in Bloom's Taxonomy are knowledge, comprehension and application. These skills are more focused on observations and ability to summarize ideas learned. They reinforce simple ideas, and are necessary to make sure that a basic understanding of a topic has been reached. But in order to progress to the higher thinking skills, (analysis, synthesis and evaluation), the ability to see things figuratively, instead of literally, becomes important. Bloom's Taxonomy provides teachers with starting words for questions in order to ensure that students are being challenged at all levels, which caters to multiple intelligences, as well as making sure that students are attempting a variety of work.

The levels of Bloom's Taxonomy are:

- Knowledge: This level tests previously learned material and may involved a wide range of materials. It relies heavily on memorization as all it requires is the appropriate information. Terms: list, define, tell, describe, identify, show, label, collect, examine, tabulate, quote, name, who, when and where.
- Comprehension: This level assesses the ability to grasp the meaning of the material learned that may be shown by interpretation and predication. Terms: summarize, describe, interpret, contrast, predict, associate, distinguish, estimate, differentiate, discuss and extend.

- Application: This is the ability to use learned information in new situations. This may be shown in the application of rules, concepts and theories. Terms: apply, demonstrate, calculate, complete, illustrate, show, solve, examine, modify, relate, change, classify, experiment and discover.
- Analysis: This level represents the ability to break down material into its parts so that its organization can be looked at. It may include the identification and labeling of its parts, analyzing these parts or recognizing how they are organized. Terms: analyze, separate, order, explain, connect, classify, arrange, divide, compare, select and infer.
- Synthesis: By putting parts together to form a new whole is the ability of synthesis tested. It may involve making a speech, a research proposal or identifying a set of abstractions. Terms: combine, modify, rearrange, substitute, plan, create, design, invent, compose, formulate, prepare, generalize and rewrite.
- Evaluation: This level tests the ability to judge the value of a material for a certain purpose. It may be based on its organization, on internal criteria, or on some external criteria; the relevance of its purpose. Terms: assess, decide, rank, grade, test, measure, recommend, convince, judge, explain, discriminate, support, conclude, compare and summarize.

Fostering higher order thinking

Firstly, it is important to set up a classroom environment that has the materials to do so. By giving students high expectations, nurturing risk-taking, grouping the students in flexible arrangements and accepting diversity, a classroom will have been created in which students feel safe to take risks and stretch their minds. It is also important to make sure that students are taking part in activities where they can communicate with others, have problems that require creative solutions, develop open-ended activities that have more than one right answer and that accommodate multiple intelligences. This way students will feel that they all have something important to contribute. The final way to incorporate higher order of thinking is to allow yourself to ask students questions to which you may not know the answer and to use a variety of assessments that will challenge all students.

Cooperative learning

Cooperative learning is using small groups that work together in order to maximize the level of every student's learning process. After receiving instruction from the teacher, small groups are organized and must complete a small task, working through the assignment as a group so that everyone knows what is going on, and then give feedback to the class as a whole or the teacher as required. When cooperative learning is done properly, all members of the group will assist each other so that everyone is able to succeed. It also works off the idea that everyone has something to learn from the other and that everyone has a role in the group. For example, if a group is putting together a PowerPoint presentation on whales, some students will be better at the research aspect, others with the technology, and some with the actual presentation.

Cooperative learning is a strategy that can be used in a classroom to increase the level of positive interdependence among students. It teaches them that everyone has strengths and when these resources are used, that everyone can benefit from them. It does not cause the students to compete against one another, but instead to focus on the positive aspects about everyone, instead of the negative ones that seem to take more importance in a competitive environment. It will also give the students many skills to use in real-life as being able to communicate effectively with others is an important life skill. Cooperative learning can increase levels of self-esteem, lead to higher levels of productivity and achievement, and create a positive classroom environment.

Just because students are assigned to work in groups does not always mean that they will work effectively. As with any other part of learning, students must be taught how to work in groups. For example, having students sit in groups while the teacher is giving a lesson could be met with competition as the students will be more likely to talk and be disruptive. Lessons must be structured cooperatively, with opportunities to work in groups as part of the structure. Choosing groups for the students ahead of time will allow the teacher to tailor the work to each group, once he knows the strengths and weaknesses of each student. It is also important to make sure that the groups are able to accomplish the learning goals set out for them and the class by tailoring the lessons accordingly.

Four ways to effectively structure cooperative learning groups are as follows:

- Positive interdependence is the most important aspect of cooperative learning. When group members sense that they are reliant on one another for success, they will realize that if they do not cooperate, then they will fail, and if they cooperate, that they will succeed.
- Having the students interact with each other by doing real work is how they can share resources, support and help each other. By going through the motions together, they will see each other's strengths and weaknesses, and support each other's learning.

- Individual and group accountability must be instilled so that students will not only feel responsible for their own contributions to the group, but also encourage others to do so.
- Students must be equipped with the necessary small group skills before attempting this type of work. It should be introduced in small doses until students know how to work together effectively.

Direct instruction

Direct instruction is defined as the procedure that is led by the teacher and is followed by the students. Students are given specific instructions as to what they are supposed to do. The teacher will introduce the task, providing background information, give the students work to complete individually, and then provide immediate feedback. The two main forms are lecturing and explaining, but could also include a question-answer session or a class discussion. By having the teacher relaying all of the information to the students, and then having the students practice the skills they have just learned, it can be easy to judge how well the students are progressing with the work.

Advantages

Direct instruction can have its advantages. If, for example, the material is simple and there is only one right answer, such as facts, then direct instruction can be the quickest and easiest way to convey this material. The teacher has control of the timing of the lesson and can make sure that it moves at a pace that is accessible to everyone. Also, the teacher has control over what will be learned and how it will be taught, so she can make it relevant to the majority of the students and cater it to the needs of the students to some degree. It is also easier to measure if the curriculum is being taught using this model of instruction because the teacher will be able to progress along a certain line of thought of teaching.

Disadvantages

Some of the disadvantages of direct instruction is that it is based on old theories of learning that believe that simple tasks must be learned before complex ones, and that the emphasis is on learning that can be quantified. This type of instruction can also minimize the prior experiences and knowledge of the individual students as the students are taught as a whole, not as individuals. Sometimes, students can lose sight of the overall task as they are caught up in the series of tasks that can make learning seem irrelevant to them. If students are not given many opportunities to do the work themselves, they can have a low retention level of what they have learned. Finally, students who learn in styles other than verbally may struggle to keep up with the lesson because various learning strategies are not catered to.

Described below is the Madeline Hunter Direct Instruction Model:
- Anticipatory Set: This should involve the bait for students to show interest in the lesson and for the teacher to focus their attention.
- Objectives: The objectives should be clear, so that the teacher knows what students will have achieved by the end of the lesson.
- Teaching: The teacher provides the information, and then shows examples of the material.
- Guided practice: Students demonstrate what they have learned through an activity supervised by the teacher.
- Checking for Understanding: The teacher may ask students questions to check understanding in order to proceed to the next level of learning.
- Independent practice: Once students have mastered the skills, more practice can be done for reinforcement.
- Closure: The teacher gives the lesson a conclusion and gives the students a chance to make sense of what they have learned.

Discovery learning

Discovery learning is a teaching approach that is based on inductive thinking. It states that students work individually in order to learn the basic principles taught in a lesson. It involves many steps, such as asking questions, exploring, and gathering data, concluding and making generalizations based upon these conclusions. Learning is solely student directed and they learn through their own experiences and thought processes. It equates the process of learning with the answer itself. Students must understand how knowledge is acquired, especially how they do it, in order to better understand information and skills. Students will rely on the teacher for guidance in case they get stuck, but it is through their own discoveries that learning takes place.

Discovery learning is defined as the process by which learning occurs through one's own efforts. In the classroom, this type of learning happens mostly through structured activities set by the teacher that require students to discover important relationships between ideas or concepts by manipulation, investigation and exploration. This requires higher-order thinking because students are provided with the minimum amount of information and then are required to formulate their own ideas for themselves. For example, students may be given a variety of objects and told to build the tallest structure, and the students must use the previous knowledge of construction to build this new object, eventually arriving at their own conclusion about what works best.

One of the advantages of discovery learning is that there is an active involvement of the learner in the learning process. Through their own experimentation and thinking will they come to the conclusion of the activity, often learning as much through the process as the end result. It also encourages curiosity and enables the students to develop life long problem solving skills. It can be highly motivating for some students as it allows them to discover their own ways to solve problems as it builds on their previous knowledge and experience. Disadvantages include that some students will find it difficult to learn without constant guidance and support. They may find it frustrating and give up easily unless a clear framework has been provided to help them find their course.

Constructivism

Constructivism is defined as a meaningful learning experience that occurs when students construct and apply their own meaning to knowledge based on their own subjective experiences and background knowledge of a topic. What is specifically challenging about constructivism is getting students to realize that they all bring preconceptions and misconceptions to the process and how to teach them to avoid doing this when it is inappropriate. By using this in the classroom, students are given the chance to participate in real-life experiences, build self-esteem by referring to previous, successful experiences, and build new thoughts through the questions asked. It is discovery-based learning and aims to make learning relevant to students and invites them to apply their previous experiences.

Reception learning

This form of learning requires the ability to receive and process structured information as received by the teacher. In order for this to effective, teacher presentations should be organized from general to specific and should use a variety of organizational tools.

This could include introductory information to give students an idea of what will be studied, descriptions of key terms and concepts they will need to know in order to progress, and a certain amount of synthesis between new material and what has already been taught. By referring to previously learned material, students will be able to see how the ideas have progressed, and have the chance to revisit older material that they might have either forgotten or not fully understood the first time it was presented.

Whole group discussion

A whole group discussion consists of the teacher and the students, where the students are usually contributing comments that are directed by the teacher. Effective whole group discussion should involve planning on the part of the teacher and the students. The teacher might outline how the discussion should develop, using key terms and ideas, and the students might think of ideas and topics to contribute to the discussion in order for it to flow smoothly. It may be helpful to have a group discussion at the beginning of a class to get ideas flowing and to summarize what information has been previously studied. It can also be the springboard into small group work or independent work.

Inequities

In a whole group discussion, it is important that the teacher sees his role as a facilitator in order to make sure that all students feel safe participating and that they all have the opportunity to do so. It is important to make sure that there are no students who are dominating the discussion and that all students have the chance to participate. If there are students who are wary of speaking in public, they could be given the chance to research what they want to say in advance so that they feel more prepared. Students should be encouraged to raise their hands, and the teacher should make sure that not one area of the room is receiving preference for contributing to make sure that all students have equal access. Alternating boy-girl-boy can be an effective way to make sure that one sex is not contributing more than the other.

Independent learning

Independent learning, or study, is the theory by which learners acquire knowledge solely through their own efforts and through this develop the ability for inquiry and critical thinking. Students must feel enabled by their teachers, meaning that they must have practice knowing how to persevere through problems on their own before asking for help from the teacher. They must be able to recognize their own faults as a learner and be held accountable for their own actions and inactions. Being exposed to effective ways to self-manage can be helpful for students who struggle working independently. Often the process of independent learning is as important as the goal of the task itself.

Students who can effectively learn independently will experience many positive side effects. Through their own processes, they will learn valuable life skills that transfer to almost any area in life. They are able to use the learning style that suits them best, and self-direction leads to higher order thinking. It mirrors learning in real life, for as adults, there will not always be someone there to guide one through life. However, there are also disadvantages to independent learning. Some students will feel discouraged by the lack of structure if they are unable to provide it for themselves. Also, some students feel that teachers should be directing them, not leaving them up to their own devices. There may be a low number of students in a classroom who are actually naturally self-directing, and the rest expect to be told what to do.

Teacher's role

Even though independent learning seems to imply that the teacher is absent from the learning process, the teacher actually plays a very important role in the process. The learning environment created by the teacher must be supportive and encouraging in order for the students to feel safe experimenting and using their imagination when learning. It is also important that there is a positive relationship between the teacher and the students in order for the teacher to help students acquire a base of knowledge from which they can then direct their own learning. The teacher must ensure that students are ready to work independently, and scaffold the learning of those who need more assistance. Finally, teaching and modeling of skills must be done in order for the students to see what they can accomplish. Some students will need to see possible outcomes before they will accomplish a task on their own.

Interdisciplinary instruction

Interdisciplinary instruction is when students are taught, and able to understand, the underlying relationships that connect what is taught in each subject. When the objectives of the lessons are clearly connected, then the higher the level of student learning is likely to occur. For example, in an art class, students might be looking at the art of a specific time period that is also being discussed in history class. By having the same time period studied in two different classes, there is a higher chance that students will see the connections and retain the information. Interdisciplinary instruction also allows students to learn the information multiple times, and the very repetition of the material will improve the learning of the students alone.

Lessons

There are several ways to develop interdisciplinary lessons. The first is to ensure that the objectives of the lesson are clear at the beginning of the lesson. This will clarify the goal of the lesson and make sure that the teacher is clear as to what the students should be learning. Second is selecting the content that will serve as the basis for the lesson, whether it be literature or a scientific principle. Third, identify other disciplines that related to the original idea, either with colleagues or on your own. Often natural links will occur, but asking other teachers will give a fresh perspective on the idea. Lastly, determine how the two or more disciplines correspond with the objectives in mind. It is important that a goal is always in sight, as with so much information it can be easy for that to become unclear.

Instruction

Three ways in which interdisciplinary instruction can take place are: thematic units, curricular connections and thinking skills development. With thematic units, the teachers organize their lessons around a specific theme, such as teamwork, respect, or fear. Teachers of objective subjects, such as math, may find it difficult to do this, but a solution can always be found. Curricular connections could work when teachers of different classes want to focus on many aspects of one idea. They may plan to do this at the same time, or one after the other in order to link the ideas. Using thinking skills development can occur when teachers want students to use the same strategies in a variety of subjects. As long as students receive adequate instruction, it can be a valuable way to instill certain strategies.

Concept mapping

Concept mapping is used by teachers when they want to represent knowledge, ideas or facts in graphs or visual organizers. They can be divided up into a variety of categories. Concepts and links can be labeled, depending on how specific the information is. Ideas work off of each other and these maps can show the relationships between a variety of concepts that might not have been immediately clear. It can be done to brainstorm before a task is started,

convey complex ideas, design a complex structure, assess understanding, measure where knowledge has not taken place, or aid learning by mixing both old and new knowledge. Meaningful learning is defined as the combining of old concepts and new concepts into existing cognitive patterns, something that can occur readily in concept mapping.

Inquiry method

Inquiry method implies that involvement in learning leads to understanding. It involves possessing and developing skills that allow you to find solutions to problems and issues while you are building on the knowledge you already possess. It is more than just asking questions and having a teacher respond. It involves several factors, such as a context existing where questions can be asked, a structure to the questions, and different levels of questions. It allows multiple intelligences to be learned because each learner can formulate their questions based on their own experiences in solving the problem. Taking data and putting into useful knowledge is a complex process, and involving students in this process will only make them more adept learners.

Inquiry based learning can be used alongside many other educational learning theories. It is a part of multiple intelligence work because it reinforces the fact that all students learn differently and provides them with opportunities to learn in the best way for them. Cooperative learning can also be used in conjunction with it as it sometimes relies on working with groups or pairs and fostering a positive rapport amongst group members in order for everyone to succeed. Finally, using inquiry method is also a key tool for how learning occurs in constructivism because the personal experiences are a part of how we construct our idea of the world around us. New experiences may cause us to change our mental rules and our preconceived notions may be altered.

Advantages

Advantages of inquiry method learning include that students are able to see how activities within a certain subject relate to other subjects; for example, persevering through a grammar problem can encourage them to try the same approach when solving a math problem. Students who participate in making observations as well as collecting, analyzing, and synthesizing information are developing useful problem-solving skills. They are also using higher order level thinking skills as they take information learned in a variety of subjects and come to their own conclusions. By developing minds that are used to inquiry methods, students will develop critical and creative thinking skills that will benefit them in real life experiences and enable them to think for themselves.

Critical perspectives

Inquiry learning has been deemed as impractical by some because it requires so much time to take place. Since each learner can move at his own pace and needs input from the teacher, it can be difficult to regulate. Some think it is more effective for students to be given the information that they will need to know in order to survive once they leave school. Students must pass tests in order to prove their knowledge, and it is often not the type of learning acquired through inquiry that is on these tests. Emphasis in education should be on a core knowledge that is similar to all students of that age. These can be found in sequenced curriculums that tend to focus on facts and other quantitative knowledge that is able to be tested and assessed more readily.

Questioning

Teachers often use questioning as a means of teaching a particular lesson, and often follow the IRE method, which states to Initiate, Respond and Evaluate. Using this, teachers follow Bloom's taxonomy of understanding to initiate (ask a question), allow the students to respond, and then to evaluate the quality of the students' responses.

Probing questions

Prompts used during interviews assist respondents in answering the interview questions. For example, when asked what he liked about being a health educator, a respondent said, "I like feeling like I help people." The interviewer used the follow-up probing question, "How do you think you have helped people as a health educator?" to get a more specific response. It is possible to get someone to look at something in a different way than before.

Play and learning

Play is a natural, fun and motivating way for children to learn, as it is the method by which they learned originally. During early childhood, children observe during play, and acquire a knowledgebase for their world through this mechanism. As such, young children should be allowed to play as part of any curriculum so as to mimic their natural learning environment.

Learning centers

When gathering ideas for a learning center, it is important that the topic is chosen carefully. It should be used to complement a topic already studied in the classroom. Then all the resources available should be gathered, including videos, books, with as much variety in the format of the texts as possible. Once all the resources are gathered, possible activities should be planned and developed, requiring that the tasks are completed independently and with the objective of the task clear. Enough time should be provided so that the students are able to complete the tasks within an acceptable amount of time. Next, create a self-grading check sheet so that the students are able to record their progress through the learning centers. As soon as everything has been put together it is time for the students to complete the tasks. The final step is to complete an evaluation, including a self-evaluation completed by the students.

Small group work

Small group work is defined as a small group of students who work together in order to complete a task or a series of tasks. When students work in small groups effectively, they tend to understand the subject matter more expansively. It helps students practice social skills, problem solving and communication skills in order to complete the task. They can be beneficial for shyer students who feel more comfortable speaking in front of small groups rather than in front of the entire class. Group work enables students to work at both the lower level and higher level orders of thinking as they often have to summarize, apply and synthesize their knowledge together in order to be successful. Students are also able to move at their own pace, and receive directions from peers in order to improve their learning.

Ineffective groups

The two main ways that affect the effectiveness of small groups is that they don't fully listen to one another and that the group members label each other. When group members don't listen to one another, they might tend to just believe that one person has all the right answers instead of thinking that everyone's viewpoint and ideas are valid. When people are labeled it can make other members feel that their opinion is not important, but to instead rely on a few to do the work for the entire work if they are not entrusted with a task to complete. They might label the "brainy" student and have him do all the thinking, and not let the "slacker" complete any of the work in fear that he will mess up. By mixing up the roles of the group, it gives

each member a chance to show their strengths and weaknesses, rather than just being prematurely and incorrectly labeled.

Successful groups

It is important to allow time to teach students how to work in small groups effectively, just like any other topic that is studied in the classroom. The first step is to assign students to appropriate groups of about four to five members. These can either be randomly assigned, or planned in advance to separate certain students from each other, and to mix up the social groups in the class. Making sure that the task requires group interaction is also important, otherwise one person may complete the task for the entire group if it was too easy. They should also know the purpose of the task so that they know what they should gain from working together. Having a time limit on the group also places restrictions and puts some pressure on them to complete the task.

During the time in which groups are working together, it is important that the teacher is visible throughout the classroom so that groups will stay on task, and that the progress on the groups can be checked without being too intrusive. By making sure that the content is clear and that they have no further questions, the students will be able to stay on task. If possible, sitting in on the group discussions will allow the teacher to see how the students are working together. The teacher can observe the group dynamic and see if they need any clarification or if they need any help. By reminding the students how much time they have left, it will redirect them to the task and ensure that it is completed properly and completely.

Closure

Once the task has been completed, it is useful to come back together as a large group and have the small groups present their findings. If other groups have issues with or questions about their work, the act of defending their work will also reinforce what they learned from the task. Using the board to summarize each groups finding will reinforce the ideas to the rest of the class. Sometimes having the students complete a self-reflection can be useful because it can help the teacher in planning the next small group activity. It can be comprised of a paragraph describing each individual's contribution, or a response to a variety of questions.

Project approach

The project approach is a set of teaching strategies that help teachers guide students through real world topics in an in-depth way. It is not unstructured and the task is usually well-planned. When the project approach is used in a classroom, it can be a highly motivating way to teach. Students will feel actively involved in their own learning and produce work that is of a high quality and of which they are proud. As it is often related to real-life experience, they will be able to apply their knowledge to a variety of situations, making each project completed helpful with skills that students will need once they have completed school.

Project creation

The first step is to present information to the students that will serve as the diving board for the task. This could be a story or video that introduces a new idea to the students. Then they might think of ideas they have about the topic, and write questions they would like to be able to answer in the course of the project. Next comes the field work. This could be research at a library, doing an interview, or going on a field trip. It needs to investigate one aspect of the topic more closely and allows the students to stimulate their thought process about the topic. Finally, the students need to come up with some way to convey the new knowledge they have acquired. They may be able to choose

from a list of ways, or come up with their own method.

Laptop computers in the classroom

Students may use laptops in the classroom, take them on field trips or go home with them. If they are used appropriately, laptops can help develop project-based learning and multimedia activities as students work to collect data, brainstorm or produce projects. Among the advantages of having class laptops are that:

- They are portable within the school and outside of class.
- They may be taken on field trips and used for investigations.
- They can provide immediate data processing and graphic feedback.
- Feedback and analysis that is immediate prompts next-step decision-making in the field.
- It allows files to be shared.
- The computers generate reports and projects.
- They can provide access to experts through e-mail or the Internet.

Internet use

Most students will probably have some experience using the Internet before they enter their classroom. Using the Internet alongside of an assignment can give students the chance to hone their searching skills, as well as their overall computer skills. However, there should be clear guidelines given to the students before the Internet is used, to prevent misuse. If the students are using the Internet for research, for instance, it can be helpful to compile a list of relevant websites for them to then narrow down. Making sure that there will be a meaningful result will ensure that the students see the benefits of using the Internet correctly. By giving the students control and having them work in groups, it can make the best of all students' skills and help students who are not as proficient on the computer learn from their peers.

Local experts

Often when completing a project or assignment, students struggle seeing how it will benefit them in real life, failing to see the relevance between education and working. By including local experts when teaching a concept or unit, it can make the link between how learning in school affects the job attained afterwards. For example, while teaching a unit on law, by having a lawyer come into the classroom, not only will he be able to give real life examples, but he will also be able to interact with the students, answering questions, and exposing them to a new career. Local experts can also provide extensive background information on a topic that the teacher is unable to provide, thus enriching the students' experience.

Primary documents and materials

Teachers can use primary sources, media, libraries and a host of other nontraditional media to make their lessons come alive for students, as such items provide real-world import to lessons which might otherwise seem sterile.

Field trips

Field trips, an excursion whereby students physically go and participate in an activity related to their topic of study, have been in use for a long time as a part of educational programming. However, sometimes funding limitations or time restrictions cause field trips to be taken rarely, if at all. Well-planned field trips have an important part of an education, and when used properly, can provide valuable learning experiences for the students. Field trips provide students with first-hand experience regarding the topic of study. It provides experiences that cannot be duplicated in the classroom, and provides more information than teachers can oftentimes provide. They provide the students with unique opportunities to learn that which otherwise would not be available to them. The field trip should be designed so that the students can see clearly the link between the concepts about which they are learning.

Virtual field trips

Sometimes it is not possible, with limits in funds and time, to take students on a real field trip. In these cases, all that is required is access to computers and the Internet in order to take advantage of the numerous virtual field trips that are available on the Internet. Virtual field trips are designed to be educational and entertaining and many of these sites can be included in small group work, independently, or as homework or extra credit assignments. Students can explore the sites at their own pace, often with a series of activities to complete, either right on the website, or as given by their teacher. Virtual field trips can be to museums or farms, or to the solar system or even inside a digestive system. They usually use audio and video segments, thus appealing to multiple intelligences and allowing many viewpoints.

Planning

The most important consideration is the educational value that the students will be able to gain. There should be clear learning objectives for the trip, and the trip should be developmentally appropriate for the students. When planning the sites, a place should be considered that will provide a unique learning environment for the students. Choosing a place that most students have already been to will take away the novelty of a place, and therefore researching this aspect is important. The interests of the children should also be taken into consideration. It makes no sense to pick a place, such as a pre-1900 art museum when the children in your class are mostly interested in modern art. It is best to pick places relevant to the students' interests.

Service learning

Service learning is the method of teaching, learning and reflecting that when used as a teaching methodology, fits into the category of experiential education. It combines academic classroom instruction with meaningful community service and attempts to achieve specific academic goals and objectives by putting them into the context of community service. Students learn real-life values by participating in real world activities, learning about citizenship and other personal life skills that are intangible skills. Sometimes school credit is awarded for service learning, whether it be in the form of credits or extra credit for a specific class. It requires the students to be self-reflective as they think and process their experiences in service learning.

Goals

It aims to connect theory learned in the classroom with action and experience. By having this experience occur in meaningful situations, such as direct service that is necessary and serves others, it helps the students to see the direct consequences of their actions. When students assist others, it can build their self-esteem as well as the self-esteem of those they are helping. It builds citizenship skills as the students must help in areas that are important and necessary. It also fulfills the goal of students seeing how their academic subject comes into play in the real world. By acting as volunteers, it could teach students that volunteering is important and rewarding and introduces them to new careers that they might not have considered before the experience.

Disadvantages

When students are required to do something, they often approach it because they have to and see it as something they have to get done. But, when they are able to choose whether or not they participate in something, those who do generally do so because of intrinsic reasons and those are the students who have the most to gain. If students were forced to complete some sort of service learning in order to graduate high school, for example, the problems that may arise may take away any benefits of the project. If the school does not have the resources to provide the students with good programs, then the bureaucracy can become a huge burden, and the students will feel unfulfilled if the programs are not developed effectively. Students may see the service as mandatory and required, and thus not feel excited about their choice.

Curriculum

Curriculum in education is defined as a set of courses and their contents offered by a school which can be determined by an individual school, local school district, or state. In the U.S., the basic curriculum of a school is established by each state, and the individual school districts adjust it as they see fit. It is based largely on teachers' past experience in schools, textbook manufacturers, teaching standards, and information from peers. As emphasis moves to results and test scores, curricula seem to focus on "teaching to the test" rather than to the overall educational experience of the students, and quantitative skills that cannot be easily measured. Teachers who are able to tailor their curricula to their students will feel more in control of their classrooms.

In order to develop an effective curriculum, it is important that the teachers are familiar with its intricacies so that they are able to clearly see how it will be presented in a classroom. Curriculum goals and objects should be outlined and shared with all the teachers in the same subject and perhaps even in the entire school. This will allow all teachers to learn from each other and know what skills are being developed across the school. It will also highlight certain aspects of a curriculum that failed to be developed or focused on. There should also be a variety of ways in which the skills can be taught so that teachers are able to adapt the work to the students in their classes. Ability will vary by class, so it is important that all students have the same access to the information in the curriculum.

Curriculum maps

Curriculum maps are the accumulation of all the goals, objectives and topics of the curriculum in all areas of the school. They are mapped out in order to see where they intertwine and are useful when thinking of ways for the skills to be applied in a classroom. It is also useful when comparing how the curriculum of one area, for example art, can coincide with the curriculum of history. It facilitates teachers to see how the skills develop over the course of the curriculum and when and where to scaffold the knowledge in order to focus on the key skills. This can be an excellent resource for teachers who are interested in doing cross-curricular activities or for teachers who are switching grade levels or subjects.

Assessment

Having a curriculum clearly mapped out can be the easiest way to determine which assessments would be an accurate test of the skills learned. Some assessments could include tests and be more traditional, or could range from being performances or a portfolio of all the work completed. Assessments should ensure that students are participating in a variety of activities so that they are able to display their strengths in a variety of ways. The assessments that tend to be most effective are ones that students are able to choose themselves, usually from a prescribed list by a teacher. This will ensure that the assessments are accurately testing knowledge and are not just an easy way out.

Curriculum maps, while useful for providing the entire school with knowledge on what is being completed in all areas of

the school, can also be used for a variety of other things. Curriculum maps can be a good start to an effective parent guidebook as it will inform parents what their children are completing in each class and will assist them in helping their children with the work by increasing the school-parent communication link. If the map is displayed in a bulletin board, it can help students see the links between areas of study and help them to see the big picture of education instead of individual classes. They also help teachers and administrators analyze how they are spending their instructional time and help to determine accountability.

Emergent curriculum

An emergent curriculum is different from the traditional sense of curriculum that the teacher plans before the students start school, based upon the goals of the school district or the state. An emergent curriculum builds upon the interests of the students and focuses on what they already know and what they would like to know in the future. It requires the teacher to take time getting to know the class, and it is often spontaneous and reacts to the immediate interests of a group. An emergent curriculum is often dynamic as well, changing depending on what shape the learning of the students is taking. The teacher is not seen as the expert, but as the facilitator of the students' learning experience.

Antibias curriculum

An antibias curriculum is an approach that challenges preconceived notions and is an activist approach of eliminating sociological maladies in education such as sexism, homophobia, ageism, racism, etc. By addressing issues of diversity and equity in the classroom, an antibias curriculum seeks to unlock students' potential by making them aware of all the issues in a society. Its goals are to develop students' self-identity, to help them interact with students from diverse backgrounds, foster critical thinking skills about bias, and teach students to stand up for themselves. It needs a safe classroom environment so that all these topics can be pursued, and discussions in order for students to learn from each other's experiences and backgrounds.

There are four main phases that can be explored to ensure that an antibias curriculum can be successful in the classroom. Teachers must create safe classrooms, and by doing this they must confront their own biases, learn about how students view diversity, evaluate the environment in the classroom for the messages it conveys about diversity, and identify parents who would be willing to help implement this change. The second and third phases involve the teachers' nonsystematic and systematic incorporating of activities into the classroom that teach antibias attitudes, whether these be role plays or activities. The last phase involves the students being a part of evaluating whether or not certain aspects of the classroom are antibiased, such as textbooks and other learning materials, and should involve parents in order to discuss these issues with their children, creating real life examples.

Motivation

Some ways in which teachers can motivate their students to learn are as follows:
- Ensure that students know what they are doing and how to know when they have achieved a goal in order for them to build their self-esteem and self-awareness.
- Do everything possible to satisfy the basic needs of the students, such as esteem, safety and belongingness.
- Try to encourage students to take risks in order to grow by talking up the rewards.
- Direct learning experiences toward feelings of success, in order to direct students towards individual and group achievement.
- Encourage the development of self-confidence and self-direction in students who needed help working on these qualities.
- Make learning relevant for the students by focusing on social interaction, usefulness and activity.

Managing the Learning Environment

Classroom management

Classroom management is defined as the set of rules or activities that the teacher sets for his classroom that outline effective and efficient instruction. This can range from establishing attendance and homework routines to dealing with inappropriate behavior. Some would argue that classroom management cannot be taught and that it is something that can only be learned through experience. Nonetheless, it doesn't do anyone any good to have a new teacher in a classroom with no idea of good ways to instill order in his classroom. Being organized is the first way to start off with a good classroom management program, as well as having an experienced teacher as a mentor, are usually good ways for a new teacher to overcome his fears about classroom management as he will have someone to whom to turn for help.

In order to be successful, classroom management should consist of the following:
- Positive classroom environment: Developing a friendly rapport with students from the first day onwards so that students will feel eager to come to class is important. Criticism of work should be worded by what the student has done well, and then some suggestions as to how to improve it, focusing on the positive aspects first.
- Clear standards of behavior for students: Rules should be enforced consistently so that there is no surprise as to what students should expect for misbehaving. Dealing with inappropriate behaviors

should be done so with a calm and clear demeanor.
- Student engagement: Having students engaged in the task will help with classroom management as there should be less inappropriate behaviors. Smooth transitions are also important so that there is no time in between activities for students to lose their concentration.

Some tips for daily classroom management success are:
- Ensure that students know the routines
- Always over plan for lessons
- Label materials clearly so that they do not need much further explanation
- Make sure expectations are clearly set for your students
- Discussions, debates and consequences are more effective than nagging, lecturing and threatening
- Review rules for behavior and work periodically
- Welcome students at the door
- Make sure there is plenty of opportunity for student participation
- Learn about the students' interests
- Involve students who misbehave
- Assign work ahead of time and give clear deadlines
- Color code materials in order to help organization
- Use eye contact
- Use both verbal and non-verbal ways to correct behavior
- Use humor daily
- Give your students compliments when they deserve them.

The major developers in classroom management theories are:
- B.F. Skinner—He outlined behavior modification which originated from behavioral psychology. He thought

that the best way to change students' behavior was to reward them for good behavior and remove rewards, or punish, inappropriate behavior.

- Carl Rogers—Socioemotional climate was given importance by Rogers because he thought that having positive interpersonal relationship between students and teachers would foster a positive classroom.
- Richard and Patricia Schmuck— They derived group process from social psychology and group dynamics research and put the emphasis on the teacher establishing and maintaining an effectively controlled classroom with cooperation being the key skills needed in order to have groups work effectively together.
- Lee and Marlene Canter—They viewed classroom management as establishing and enforcing classroom rules as a way of controlling student behavior, mainly by discipline.

Daily procedures, routines and rules

The most important thing to remember when dealing with students is that consistency is vital. If one student sees you deal with something in a certain way, the next student will expect the same treatment. If she is treated differently, then she will see your rules as flexible, or that they don't even matter. It is better to be tough at the beginning of the school year, and as many teachers will tell you—"Don't smile until after Christmas"—you are ultimately there in the classroom to be a teacher, not a friend to the students, and remaining firm with your rules and routines will earn their respect as well as maintain an orderly classroom. Empty threats can be especially damaging. It is best to clearly outline the consequences for misbehavior, or inability to produce class work or homework as soon as possible and then follow through.

Consequences

When deciding on rewards and consequences, it is useful to make sure that they are relevant to the students and the situation. It makes sense to punish a student who does not complete his homework by having them complete the homework in a detention after school, or having the student complete it by a certain date, otherwise the parents would be notified. It would not be appropriate, for example, to have the student stand in the hallway, when he could be in the class learning the material. When students see clear links between the consequences and their behavior, they will know their limits and be more inclined to behave appropriately or complete assignments on time.

Positive guidance

When the differences between girls and boys were looked at in many gender studies, it was found that boys tended to be more assertive and aggressive, while the girls tended to be passive. The way the teachers were dealing with the boys tended to be more verbal, thus reinforcing that calling out would get more attention than the more desirable behavior of the girls who would raise their hands and pay attention. Praising and giving compliments encourages students to focus and stay on task if they want to receive praise and attention. Ignoring misbehavior can be effective, as long as it doesn't get out of hand, at ensuring that the misbehaving students know that negative behavior will get a negative reaction, or no reaction at all. Focusing on the problems in a classroom can inadvertently be rewarding to those who misbehave and cause the negative behavior to manifest itself further.

Classroom rules

Starting off the school year with a clearly defined set of classroom rules will let your students know their limitations from the beginning. Many teachers have their students participate in the creation of the rules. Starting off by brainstorming ideas for rules may have you discover that student-created rules may be more strict that you would create yourself. Most students want to learn in a safe environment and feel better when there are defined boundaries. It is useful to create consequences after each repetition of the undesirable; for example, after the first violation, the student's name goes on the board. After the second violation, the student stands in the hallway, and after the third violation there is a note home, detention or whatever the relevant consequence may be.

The rules should be positive by nature. Some students tend to see rules that are worded negatively as a challenge and will attempt to break the rule, for example, "Raise your hand before speaking," is worded positively, whereas: "Don't call out," is worded negatively. Rules should also be worded as simply as possible, but should be well-defined in a discussion before it is decided upon. For example, if "Be respectful to others" is one of your rules, make sure the students know what respecting someone looks like by providing examples. Keeping the list short is also important because students will be more likely to keep to them if there are just a few. And lastly, enforce the rules that are created. It does no good for the students to see a rule being broken by another student who does not receive the prescribed consequences.

Classroom reward structures

The following are two types of classroom reward structures:

- Competitive goal structures: Grading that is done on a curve only allows a certain number of students to achieve at any one level, therefore any accomplishment comes at another student's expense. Students constantly feel the need to outdo one another, even focusing on each other's failures to try to get ahead. It can cause students to believe that achievement is ability based, and if they don't believe they have the ability to succeed, then they will never try to do so.
- Individual goal structures: Students work alone and earn rewards based on their individual performance. They do not concern themselves with the efforts of other students.
- Cooperative goal structures: Students work together to achieve shared goals. Since the group can only achieve well if all its members work together, then positive interdependence is important to the group.

Consequences

Consequences vs. punishment

Natural and logical consequences are often confused with punishments. Of course, teachers have wanted inappropriate behaviors of students to be stopped and have used means such as writing sentences, isolation and corporal punishment in the past in order to do so. As a result, the term punishment is negatively viewed because of the types of punishment used in the past. Using natural and logical consequences has been the result of wanting to use noninvasive consequences in order to deal with behavior. Although some would argue that only using these types of "positive" consequences does not represent real life and will leave students ill-prepared for the punishments that do exist for adults. Therefore, the most balanced classroom management policies will teach students that they have to deal with the responsibilities of their actions and are parallel with real-life situations that they may face as adults.

Natural consequences

Natural consequences are results of behavior that are not planned or controlled but the result of a behavior. For example, if a student is working and another student steals her pen, the first student will probably not lend the other student a pen in the future. Teachers do not have any control over these consequences because they are merely the natural reaction to an undesirable behavior. Teachers can, however, teach students how to predict these behaviors; for example, if a student would like to borrow money from their parents, doing something nice for them will probably cause the parent to look favorably upon their child rather than having their child show them a bad report card and then asking them for money.

Logical consequences

Logical consequences do not occur naturally due to a behavior but instead are implemented by teachers. They are similar to the consequences that an adult would face and they therefore teach students what to expect in life and should be related, respectful and reasonable. A related logical consequence means that the consequence has a clear link to the student's behavior. For this one it is important that a teacher knows his students in order to make sure that the consequences are related to each student. For example, having a consequence be an after school detention for not completing homework may be effective for a student in after-school sports, but not for a student who picks up their sisters from elementary school. Consequences need to be given respectfully so that the student understands how her behavior led to being punished. Finally, consequences should be reasonable and understood by the student.

Wasted time: This logical consequence is based on the idea that both the teacher and the students in the classroom have important jobs to do. The main reason why school exists is for learning to take place, and anyone who interferes with that is wasting time. Students should, from the beginning, see the connection between school and what they want to do with their lives. This will help them understand that when they misbehave and suffer the consequences, that it is not from the teacher but it is because of their own action or inaction. If a student is choosing to interfere with someone's job in the classroom, then she is wasting time. The teacher can give her the choice to stop wasting time and let her know that she will make it up. If the student chooses to continue, then she will lose some of her free time later in order to make it up.

Feedback

The main difference that must be outlined when giving feedback is whether the feedback is relating to the students' work or is about the students themselves. Therefore giving feedback that improves the students' self-esteem rather than damaging it is something that must be carefully defined. Some theorists in the past thought that students did better in the face of criticism because they would want to improve on their work and that would be the drive behind improvement. Constant praise was thought to only fuel under-achievement as the students thought they had already received perfection and wouldn't strive to achieve any better. It is not to say that students should never have their behavior corrected or receive any criticism, but the feedback they receive should clearly be a criticism of what the students produced, not of the students themselves.

Helpful feedback should be prompt, occur right after the event, contain encouragement for the student to do even better next time, be specific about what was positive and negative, and focus clearly on a few aspects rather than a host of different ones. If the teacher can identify the students' weaknesses, then that will help the student correct her own problems, instead of having the teacher do all the work for her. Unhelpful feedback could be generalized and vague, leaving the student with unclear feelings about what to change; giving an opinion instead of objectively pointing out problems with the work, or focused on an aspect that the student cannot change. The student should be able to hear the respect in any feedback, and in all types of feedback, fact and description should be the focus, not the personal opinion of the teacher.

Effective communication with parents

Being able to communicate effectively with parents can be the key to having a successful classroom. If parents feel that you are keeping their interests in mind when you are teaching, it will be that much easier to communicate with them when you have concerns with their children. Having parents support you at home will enforce the idea in the classroom that you are the teacher and there are certain expectations you have of the students. Communicating effectively can mean making phone calls when both positive and negative feedback about their children can be given. It is important to remember that all families have strengths to build upon, most parents really do care about their children, cultural differences are both valid and valuable, different forms of families exist and all are important, and parents have valuable perspectives about their children to share with you.

When face-to-face conferences are not possible, there are many other ways to communicate. With regard to telephone calls, the first should be introductory and positive, as it will set a precedent for all other calls that you will make, in that you do not only call when there is something negative that happened. As with all forms of communication, it is helpful with parents to maintain a level of respect and cordiality. Phone calls, emails, newsletters and class websites are all ways to ensure that parents know how to contact the teacher if there are problems. It is important to keep a record of all communications with parents and to ensure that they feel as comfortable contacting you as you feel about contacting them. With phone calls, try to have something both positive and negative with which to talk about, in order to refer to them in subsequent communication.

Most parents will appreciate communication from the classroom and its daily routines. A classroom website could be helpful if they are computer literate, otherwise a monthly or weekly newsletter could be just as effective. Possibilities for either's content could include: announcements of upcoming events or class trips, reminders about homework or other deadlines with projects, list of items needed for class projects (presentation boards, folders, etc), descriptions of units and ways to continue learning at home, lists of homework assignments or other work students could complete at home for enrichment, explanations of class rules and behavior standards as well as consequences, outlines of grading policies and other assessments, or resources in the community that will complement any work done in the classroom, such as museum exhibits or plays.

Reasons for misbehavior

The following are four reasons why students misbehave in school:

- Attention: Some students feel that they belong in a classroom only when they are being noticed, whether this be by a teacher or fellow student. Giving positive attention to these students will ensure that they do not resort to negative behavior in order to obtain it.
- Power: Some students want to be in control. It is important to ensure

that consequences are clear and followed so that the students do not completely disregard them.

- Revenge: There will be some students who will hurt other students. Encouraging students and fostering a safe classroom environment will ensure that no students feel the need to hurt others or themselves.
- Inadequacy: When students have a low self-esteem or self-worth, they don't believe that they can succeed at anything and will develop feelings of inadequacy and misbehave to distract attention from the fact that they struggle at classroom tasks.

Classroom arrangement

Well-run classrooms often begin with the physical layout of the space; how well the desks are arranged and how easily accessible the materials and supplies are to the teacher and the students. The arrangement of your classroom will reflect your teaching style. For example, if you want a lot of small cooperative group work, then make sure that the desks are in small clusters around the room. If you tend to have more large-group discussions, then having the desks in a U-shape so that everyone is visible is the best way to organize the room. However, the most important aspect is making sure that all materials are organized and accessible to you. There should also be a cupboard or shelf with materials that students can access easily to avoid asking you and interrupting the lesson, or waiting in line instead of commencing their work.

Environmental features
Temperature, lighting and noise level are all important environmental features that are a part of your classroom. These three, if controlled properly, can have a large influence on your classroom management.

Lighting is important because if it is too bright, it can cause some students to be restless or hyperactive. If possible, having lamps in one area to create a dimly-lit reading area with chairs, plants and cushions could be helpful if the resources are available to you. As for the noise level, have the students demonstrate what good noise levels are by some demonstrations. Temperature is something over which teachers often have no control, but making sure that students dress appropriately is a good way to be proactive.

Course content and material

Texts and reading should be chosen with gender-neutral language, free of stereotypes. Texts that do include these should be addressed and discussed. The curriculum should be inclusive by including the perspectives and experiences of a pluralistic society. All points of view should be presented so that no one view takes precedence over the others. When making references to culture or history, make sure that your students are given background information and the opportunity to ask for clarification. Do not assume that all of your students will be able to pick up on these references. Considering students needs when assigning homework is also considerate based on the different family structures at home. If requiring the use of a computer, make sure that opportunities to use computers at school are permitted in the case of students who do not have access to one at home.

Behavioral objectives

A behavioral objective is a clear and unambiguous description of the expectations for the students that will set out which behaviors are acceptable and which behaviors are not. There are usually three parts of a behavioral objective: student behavior, conditions of performance, and performance criteria. Student behavior outlines the skill or knowledge that should be gained as well as the result that the students will be able to accomplish. The conditions of performance is under what circumstances or in what situation the students will be able to perform the behavior, such as in an oral presentation, or with note cards. Finally, performance criteria is how well the individual behavior is done, compared to a standard that is outlined to the students.

Behavioral objectives appear in the cognitive, affective and psychomotor domains:

- Cognitive Domain: These objectives will refer to intellectual learning and problem solving as the cognitive levels are knowledge, comprehension, application, analysis, synthesis and evaluation.
- Affective Domain: The affective domain refers to the emotional and value system of students. These are learned by receiving, responding, valuing, organizing, and characterizing a value. It could be an objective for students to be able to receive constructive criticism and to better their performance.
- Psychomotor Domain: This refers to movement characteristics and capabilities and could be used as a way for students to use different ways in order to present their information. It involves the use of motor skills, whether small or gross, and can add a three dimensional aspect to the way students learn.

Learner objectives and outcomes

Objectives make the course provide focused, consistent, and clear evaluation criteria. With clear objectives, students will know what to expect and what is expected of them. Students should be able to see what they will be able to do differently at the end of a unit or a specific task if the objectives are set out in advance.

There are three things that should be considered when creating learner objectives: First, the focus of the class should be outlined so that students know what they will learn during its course. If the course is consistent in sticking with these objectives, then the students will respond well to the structure and feel that they have control over what they are learning. Students should also understand the criteria by which they will be graded, and know how to improve their performance if they so desire.

Learner objectives should be specific and clear so that the student knows exactly what is expected. If the objectives are clear, then they should be able to be assessed in some way that can be quantified, such as giving a time limit to work on a project, or a page or word limit. As with this, the students should have some say as to whether or not the task is acceptable, so if possible, there should be some choice within the task so that the students will find the task doable and realistic. Having a time frame is also a good way to make sure that the task is realistic, and especially with longer projects, giving goals, such as writing five pages of a thirty page paper each week, can help students to structure their time more wisely.

General learner outcomes are the goals that are set for all grade levels and in all academic disciplines. They aim to help the students live productive and enriching lives. There are seven general learner outcomes. To be a self-directed learner gives one the ability to be responsible for his own learning. A community contributor understands that it is vital that humans are able to work together. Being a complex thinker means that one has the ability to demonstrate critical thinking and problem solving skills. A quality producer has the ability to recognize when one's efforts are of quality and is able to reproduce that level of work in the future. Being an effective communicator is also important in order to work well with others, and lastly, being an effective and ethical user of technology is important as well because technology is used more and more often.

Guided practice

Guided practice can be used in situations where the teacher wants to monitor student progress. It is usually an activity that provides students the opportunity to grasp and develop concepts or skills that have just been taught to them. This is usually something that is done individually so that the teacher is able to assess how well the students have grasped the concepts before moving on to the next topic. However, it is not just simply worksheets, or questions; it is applying the knowledge to activity that encourages the students to use higher level of thinking in order to show that they have learned the skills and ideas presented to them. It can be used to check understanding and to monitor how well the students have mastered the topic. The teacher will also be able to help students who are struggling with a certain aspect before moving on, as the teacher is helping students individually.

The teacher would introduce a topic and after doing a few practice items, the guided practice would begin. It holds each student individually accountable by having them show that they are able to do and understand the work. The teacher will be continuously moving around the room in order to check that the students are on task and working through the task correctly, as well as giving assistance to students who need it. If students are not monitored correctly, there runs the chance of some students not grasping a task that will be built on at the next step, thus causing frustration and apathy. That is why it is important that the activity set requires individual effort that can be accurately monitored by the teacher as he is walking around the room, and does not consist of multiple choice or true/false questions.

Independent practice

Independent practice occurs when skills and strategies have been taught in the classroom as a part of a unit or activity. Practice follows once an activity has been set and the teacher has observed the students independently working in order to judge whether or not the skill has been learned. Independent practice takes place when new skills are to be applied in familiar formats and judges whether or not students are able to apply new information. For example, if students are learning about division, the teacher may teach long division by starting out with smaller numbers, and then give the students problems that contain more numbers than taught to see if they are able to apply the information effectively.

Homework

Homework is generally the time that students spend outside of the classroom completing assigned activities such as practices, reviews or applied skills learned in the classroom. It enables students to work independently therefore improving independent study skills. Homework can provide more practice time for tasks that students find challenging and extend the knowledge of students who have already grasped the material. It can assist teachers in knowing how the students are progressing with the material, and help them to help students who are struggling. If students are held accountable for the work they do, it helps them to become more responsible and accountable for their work. It can also be a time to engage the parents in the work and encourage parents to take part in their students' education, as well as knowing that the school has high expectations for each student.

Homework should never be seen as a punishment, so giving students "no homework" as a reward should be avoided. Make sure that the homework assignments are varied by having some be short term and others being long term. Having homework assignments that take too long to be completed should be avoided so that students don't see homework as a constant frustration. If links are made to class work and homework, then students will see homework as important to the class and do it more regularly. Instructions should be clear as well as the consequences for late or incomplete homework. It should be corrected in a timely manner so that students will be able to track their progress and should also include feedback so students will know how they can improve.

At the beginning of the year, it is helpful to have a handout for parents on the expectations in the classroom, as well as with homework. In this way they will know what is to be expected and can assist their children as needed. Also including some tips such as how to set up a good study environment and ways for the parent to help with the homework can be good things to include as well. When the first instances of incomplete or late homework occur, it is important to contact parents as soon as possible so that the parents will realize that homework is important to the class. Having a homework diary or someplace, like in the back of a notebook, where the students keep a list of homework can help parents know what is expected of their children and enable to help them accordingly.

Transitions

Transitions are periods of time in which the activity moves from one stage to another. It could be the time period between when a teacher assigns a task to when the students actually start the task, or the time period between when the students enter the room and when they are sitting at their desks. Successful transitions require many things, including careful planning, teaching, monitoring and feedback. How to deal with transitions needs to be taught to the students just as any other classroom routine. For example, having a list of things

for students to do after they finish a task before the other students can stop problems with behavior if they always know that there is something for them to do. Most students will respond well to knowing the structures for transitions, especially since there are so many on a daily basis that they will encounter.

Setting teaching routines is an important way to teach transition skills because it lets the students know what is expected of them. By modeling both incorrect and correct examples of what to do, the students can see clearly what is expected. Also, making sure that the teacher reminds students what to do before the transition occurs will refresh their memory and give them a chance to succeed. It is important, however, not to do this all the time, as students will always expect to have a warning instead of just sensing the transition. When students to engage in appropriate behavior, having incentives and specific praise should be given. By recognizing appropriate behavior and ignoring or directing inappropriate behavior, students will know what to do. Finally, by having the teacher actively scanning the classroom, and moving around, students will feel the need to stay on task because they know they are being monitored.

Exploration in the classroom

Exploration is a valuable skill to encourage in the classroom because it will often lead to higher levels of productivity and satisfaction with work, as students will have had more influence on the results. As long as exploration is encouraged regardless of the result, students will feel comfortable trying new things. Students should feel safe as they are experimenting. Constantly trying to guide their behavior, which a teacher may see as being helpful, could restrict their work because most of the time what students come up with will be much different than what the teacher foresaw. Praising small advances is also important because if the teacher acts disappointed as students try and fail, they will be less willing to try new tasks. Having the task to be completed broken up into small, doable tasks is a better way to encourage success.

Assessment

Quantitative and performance-based measurements

A quantitative measurement uses results from an instrument based on a standardized system that limits the collection of data to a preset amount of possible responses. This is more commonly known as a standardized test, such as the ACT or SAT to get into college, or any test with multiple choice responses. This type of measurement is more concerned with the details of performance and can be used as both a pre-and post-subject assessment of performance after knowledge on a certain topic has been studied. When these tests are given in the classroom, they can be more effective if a more experienced teacher has created the test in order to ensure that concepts are being tested, not just facts and ideas.

Performance-based assessments are concerned with problem solving and understanding. The goal of this type of assessment is that students should be able to show their understanding of a topic studied that falls in line with certain curriculum goals. These types of assessment can provide a measure of achievement as well as track a teacher's progress with an individual student. They could take the form of essays, oral presentations, open-ended problems, role-playing or hands-on tasks. It could also take the form of a portfolio that students put together throughout the study of a certain topic that shows how their learning has taken place over a period of study. Self-evaluation also has a place in performance-

based assessment as the students often have to be critical of themselves and the process it took them to get to the finished result.

Both types of assessment have their place in the classroom, as long as they are used accurately. It would not be useful, for example, to have a multiple-choice test after having students read a book in order to show their interpretation of a book. It would, however, be appropriate to have a standardized test regarding vocabulary or the background to a novel, to then be taken after the text to see how much the students have learned. Performance-based assessment tends to be more individually driven by each student and by that fact alone it tends to be a more exciting form of assessment. However, it requires a lot of thought on the teacher's part in order to make sure that all the choices are relevant to the topic and can be graded on some sort of scale.

Testing modifications

The following are some considerations when making testing modifications:

- Directions: Key words could be underlined by the teacher, or the teacher could read the directions aloud and ask if there are any questions before beginning.
- Adapted Expectations: The grading scale could be altered to account for students with lower cognitive functioning that may know some of the concepts, but not all of them.
- Time constraints: Extended test time with supervision could be determined to be appropriate depending on the student and his IEP.
- Essay questions: Completing an outline could be an option, or having the student verbalize answers onto a tape recorder, or having someone else transcribe his answers.

- Additional tools: For some tests, formulas, sample problems, dictionaries or computers may be used in order to facilitate the test-taking process.

Strategies

An assessment is an illustrative task or opportunity to perform that targets the educational objectives for an assignment and allows students to demonstrate what they have learned and the progress of their learning. There are many strategies that can be used as strategies to assess student learning. Graphic organizers can allow the presentation of a variety of information or show how the information was obtained and learned. Interviewing others can provide a real life experience to a topic studied in class and put a face to the story and experience. Doing an observation can help students see how the topic appears in real life. If students complete self or peer evaluations, these can be useful because sometimes feedback from a peer group is more valuable than that of a teacher. Finally, portfolios can contain a little bit of everything and can track how the students have progressed through the assessment.

Rubrics

Assessment rubrics are authentic assessment tools that are used to measure the work of students. It aims to evaluate a student's performance based on a set of criteria related to the task, rather than giving a single score for the work. Students usually receive the rubric before they attempt the task so that they know what is expected and for them to think about how the criteria will play out in their work. They can be analytic or holistic and are tailored to individual assessment tasks, allowing teachers to design the rubric for individual classes and the needs of the students. Rubrics are also a formative type of assessment because it is an ongoing part of the teaching and learning process since it

is revealed to the students before the assessment is even commenced.

Standard deviation

Standard deviation is a measure of the range of values in a set of numbers and it is a statistic used as a measure of the dispersion or variation in a distribution, equal to the square root of the arithmetic mean of the squares of the deviations from the arithmetic mean. The standard deviation of a random variable or list of numbers (the lowercase Greek sigma) is the square root of the variance. The standard deviation of the list [x1, x2, x3] with a mean value of 5 is given by the formula:

$$\sigma = \sqrt{\frac{(x_1 - 5)^2 + (x_2 - 5)^2 + (x_3 - 5)^2}{3}}$$

In this formula, sigma (the standard deviation) is equal to the square root of the variance, which is given as the sum of each value minus the mean, squared, divided by the total number of values. This formula is used when all of the values in the population are known. If the values x1...xn are a random sample chosen from the population, then the sample Standard Deviation is calculated with same formula, except that (n-1) is used as the denominator.

Grade equivalent score

What the grade equivalent score actually measures is how typical students at the grade level specified would perform on the test that has been given. In other words, a 4th grader's grade equivalent of 10.4 does not indicate that the 4th grade is capable of doing 10th grade work. Rather, it indicates that the 4th grade student has performed as well as a typical 10th grade student would have performed on the 4th grade test. If the student is performing on grade level, that is a 4th grade student taking the test in the 10th month of 4th grade receives a score of 4.10, then it simply indicates that he/she is performing right at the average for other

4th graders in the norming sample, which is the 50th percentile and 50th NCE. Grade equivalents do not lend themselves to measuring aggregate performance of all students in a school or school district, nor do they average well and are hard to understand when dealing with groups. Accordingly, the score used more often is the Normal Curve Equivalent, or NCE.

Important terms

- Standard error of measurement - The estimate of the 'error' associated with the test-taker's obtained score when compared with their hypothetical 'true' score. The SEM, which varies from test to test, should be given in the test manual. The band of scores in which we can be fairly certain the 'true' score lies can be calculated from this figure.
- Raw score - is an original datum that has not been transformed. A standard score is a dimensionless quantity derived from the raw score.
- Scaled score - is a standardized score, that is, it is based upon the normal distribution and standard deviation units.
- Mastery levels - The cutoff score on a criterion-referenced or mastery test; people who score at or above the cutoff score are considered to have mastered the material; mastery may be an arbitrary judgment.

Collaboration, Communication, Professionalism and Language Arts

Effective communication techniques

Two main ways to ensure generally effective communication techniques involve listening actively and controlling the nonverbal message that is being sent to the speaker. When listening, remain attentive and concentrate on what is being said. Also, don't form an opinion right away; be impartial in order to take the most away from what is being said. Reflecting on that which is being said can be done by restating the message so that the speaker knows that you understand. Summarizing what the speaker has said will also show that you have paid attention to the details. The nonverbal message conveyed is also important. You should be aware of your body posture and the level of eye contact you are using. Staring students directly in the eye could be seen as confrontational, whereas complete lack of eye contact can be viewed as disinterest. If you are speaking to a student, try to have a parallel body position, either both be standing or sitting in order to put you both on an equal level.

Nonverbal communication

Nonverbal communication is the set of ways in which humans send and receive messages without using words. For teachers, it is just as important to be effective nonverbal communicators as verbal communicators. They are essential aspects of the teaching process and can sometimes even be more effective than a verbal reminder. Nonverbal communication includes gestures, facial expressions, proximity, humor, posture, body orientation or touching. Being aware of the ways the students communicate nonverbally can also assist teachers in getting messages about how their students are learning. Sometimes sending signals can reinforce learning more effectively, because they are implicit and students will learn how to react to your nonverbal communication more readily because it tends to be less confrontational than direct statements.

Four commonly used types of nonverbal communication are eye contact, facial expressions, gestures, and body orientation. Eye contact helps to regulate the flow of communication between two people as well as registering interest in the topic at hand. Teachers who use eye contact convey warmth, concern and directness. Facial expressions are nonverbal communicators that have been taught to us since birth to convey a wide range of emotions. For instance, smiling conveys happiness, warmth, friendless and liking. If teachers smile often, then students will tend to react positively and develop a better feeling toward the class and sometimes even learn more effectively. Gestures can include movements with hands that sometimes serve no larger purpose than entertainment or to keep attention, but can also help an instructor illustrate valuable concepts. Body orientation conveys the message that you are either interested or disinterested in the person speaking to you; leaning forward is more favorable of a position than reclining back in ones chair.

Three other aspects of nonverbal communication include proximity, paralinguistics and humor. Proximity is usually set out by the cultural norms regarding space. When a student is not focusing, sometimes standing next to his desk is just as effective as verbally reminding him to pay attention. Usually having the teacher walk around the room increases interaction with the students. Paralinguistics are the vocal elements of nonverbal communication, such as tone, pitch, rhythm, loudness and inflection. Teachers who speak in a monotone voice tend to be perceived as boring because there is no variety. But, when teachers use variety in their voice, it tends to keep the interest of the students longer. Humor can also be a useful teaching tool because it can release stress and tension for both the teacher and students. It can foster a friendly classroom environment that facilitates learning, and as long as it is used appropriately, is very useful and effective.

Gender-neutral language

Gender neutral language is language that attempts to not refer to either males or females when coming up with examples where the sex of the person involved cannot be determined. For example, when teaching occupations, make sure that all occupations are either male or female, such as chair instead of chairman. It is preferable to avoid regendering terms; therefore chair is preferable to chairwoman if the person being referred to is a woman. Creating gender neutral terms is also effective, as is avoiding terms that have – ette and –ess endings, as those tend to be derogatory.

Understanding and factual recall

Repeating key terms or concepts frequently is preferential. The more often students hear something, the more likely they will be to remember it later. Thus, reviewing key concepts often is going to be most effective. Providing students with visual aids to reinforce and explain abstract concepts is going to be more important as today's students tend to be visual learners. Encourage students to use logical thinking when necessary by pointing out which information is fact and which exists logically. This will help students apply knowledge in new situations more readily. By using in-class activities to reinforce newly presented materials, one will allow students to show what they have learned.

Having students give feedback about what they have learned will also increase their understanding.

Convergent thinking

Convergent thinking is that which represents the analysis or integration of already taught or previous knowledge. It leads one to an expected end result or answer. It usually involves the terms explaining, stating relationships, and comparing and contrasting. The way it is structured may differ, but the expected result will be a justified answer to the topic. Questions to rouse convergent thinking usually begin with why, how or in what ways. These ensure that the thinking is led in a certain direction with the answer always in mind. Using these question tags effectively will require specific events or people so that the students know what the expected answer should involve.

Divergent thinking

Divergent thinking is generating many ideas about a topic in a short period of time. It stems from the idea that there is not one right idea, but that many ideas are possible. It involves taking one topic and breaking it down into many smaller parts in order to gain insight about the topic as a whole. Divergent thinking usually occurs in spontaneous, free-flowing ways because the ideas that create this type of thinking often are thought of in these patterns as well. The ideas may then be put back together in a more structured way in order to be understandable to the other students. It can be an effective way for students to start a new topic, as divergent thinking will allow them to examine what they already know about the topic.

Two ways to stimulate divergent thinking are brainstorming and keeping a journal. Brainstorming involves making a list of ideas in a creative, yet unstructured way. Its goal is to generate as many ideas as possible in a short period of time. It often relies on one idea to spawn the process of thinking in a variety of directions. During brainstorming, all ideas are seen as important and no idea is disregarded or criticized. They are all seen as important because of the thought process. After brainstorming is complete, only then can the list be reviewed and the best ideas sorted out from the rest. Keeping a journal is also an effective way to record ideas on a daily basis. It can take the form of a small notebook, or just a piece of paper on which to jot ideas. This is useful because students sometimes will gather inspiration at unusual times and places, and by always having a journal handy, it can be ensured that the ideas do not go to waste.

Free writing and mind- or subject-mapping are two others ways that can stimulate divergent thinking. Free writing is when a student focuses on one particular topic and writes non-stop about it for a short period of time. It could be on an idea that was spawned during brainstorming, or on a new unit in a class. It is useful to generate a variety of thought on a topic that can then be used for later work in the unit once it is restructured or put into a logical order. Finally, mind- or subject-mapping involves taking all the brainstormed ideas and putting them into a visual organizer that shows the relationship between the ideas. It may start with a central theme, and then show all the topics related to the theme and their subtopics.

Motivation through communication

Assist students by creating a link when you are teaching something new. If students can see how it relates to something that they have previously been taught, then the odds of learning the new material are increased. Vocabulary is something to be considered, both what the teacher uses and what the students use. It should be introduced with a real-life definition and with many opportunities for the students to use the words. Students should be

communicated with respectfully and addressed appropriately for the setting in order for them to reciprocate respect. Finally, communicating that students are held to high standards right from the start will let them know what is to be expected and for them to keep striving for their best.

Caring community

A caring community is the way in which the school interacts with the surrounding neighborhood and town. In such a community, all families are welcome and the immediate area is seen in the spirit of cooperation between the students and their families. The populations of students who attend a school will tend to be diverse, and therefore all families should feel included in the community of the school. Individual students will feel included if they are treated well by the staff and their fellow students and feel that the staff has concern for their well being, and that they are valued. In order for this to work, students must feel that their input and participation is a necessary function of the school and that there is communication between all facets of the school and the community. Family and staff members work together to solve problems and the rights of all students are strictly upheld.

Constructing a caring environment in the classroom from the beginning means that insults and derogatory terms are eliminated so that students feel safe in the environment. Students should treat the teacher with courtesy and respect, and that should be reciprocated. Having interactions between students on a regular basis will increase the level of community in the classroom because students will get to know each other and not use prejudice readily. When appropriate, if the students have the chance to provide their input into that which they study, they will feel motivated to learn and share their knowledge with others. Balancing between teacher-centered and student-centered

- 56 -

activities will spread out the activities and make students feel accountable for their own learning. Setting an appropriate way to deal with behavior will also increase the sense of community, in that students feel that they are being dealt with appropriately. This works reciprocally, as well, in that pre-set consequences for actions which are enforced fairly and regularly create a stable environment.

Important terms

- Ethnocentrism - The inability to accept another culture's world view.
- Discrimination - Differential treatment of an individual due to minority status, whether actual or perceived.
- Stereotyping - Generalizing how a person is to be treated, while ignoring the fact that individual differences occur.
- Cultural Blindness - Differences in culture or language are ignored as though the differences did not exist.
- Cultural imposition - The belief that everyone should conform to the majority.

Professional development resources

Types of resources available for professional development and learning are:

- Professional literature - books and publications are examples of literature that can help a classroom teacher.
- Colleagues - a fellow member of a profession, staff, or academic faculty; an associate
- Professional Associations - an association of practitioners of a given profession, for example NEA, NSTA, etc.
- Professional development activities – sometimes put on by a local or state school board to teach

educators the newest trends in education.

Professional development and maintenance

Teachers should continually keep up to date with the newest research with regard to teaching theory, and be able to understand and apply this information so as to remain current and professionally prepared to do one's job. Many professional literature sources are available online, and allow one to put the most effective teaching methods into practice.

Code of ethics

Ethical codes are specialized and specific rules of ethics. Such codes exist in most professions to guide interactions between specialists with advanced knowledge, e.g., doctors, lawyers and engineers, and the general public. They are often not part of any more general theory of ethics but accepted as pragmatic necessities. Ethical codes are distinct from moral codes that apply to the education and religion of a whole larger society. Not only are they more specialized, but they are more internally consistent, and typically can be applied without a great deal of interpretation by an ordinary practitioner of the specialty.

Student advocacy

Public support for education is fragile. Poverty jeopardizes the well-being and education of our young people and some communities are caught in a downward spiral of cynicism and mistrust. Teachers must necessarily be advocates for education. One might become involved in efforts to change policies, programs, and perceptions to benefit learners; such involvement is crucial for educators today, for when they do not create effective channels of communication with legislators, the media, and community members, their opinions will very likely go unfulfilled legislatively. These consequences can be devastating to children and to learning. The stakes are simply too high for educators not to engage in advocacy efforts. Just as teaching and learning require commitment, energy, and perseverance, so too does advocacy.

School as a community resource

Our mission is to work with communities to ensure learner success and stronger communities through family-school-community partnerships. Through schools, individuals value learning; learn how to learn; demonstrate effective communication, thinking and problem solving; enjoy a better quality of life; are fulfilled; experience the joy of learning; and contribute to and benefit from the intergenerational transmission of culture. In supporting the educational role and function of local education agencies (and organizations), families, and communities increase local capacity to improve and ensure learning opportunities for the children and citizens of the community.

Partnerships with families and communities

When schools and families work together to support learning, everyone benefits: students perform better in school and in life, parents become empowered, teacher morale improves, schools get better and communities grow stronger. Educators sometimes are content to let parents and families take the initiative in becoming involved in their children's education. But for a real partnership to occur, educators must look at ways in which the school can initiate this involvement. In such a partnership, the school and the home share responsibility for children's learning; the relationship is based on mutual respect and acknowledgment of the assets and expertise of each member. As an extension of this partnership, schools can emphasize a

broad base of community involvement. When schools develop and implement strategies for promoting effective school-family-community partnerships, the result is improved learning for all students and strengthened schools, families, and communities.

Parental involvement

Increased involvement of parents and families often is cited as one of the most important ways to improve public schools. A variety of studies confirm that parent involvement makes an enormous impact on students' attitude, attendance, and academic achievement. Although some working and single parents may be unable to contribute to schools because of work commitments and time constraints, educators are discovering many additional ways that parents can help students and their schools. Some of these ways are dependent upon the school's desire to involve parents. To effect change, parents must find time to participate in their children's education while schools must provide the supports necessary for them to be involved. The resulting partnerships between parents and teachers will increase student achievement and promote better cooperation between home and school. Together these efforts will connect families and schools to help children succeed in school and in their future. Traditionally, parent involvement in education has included home-based activities (such as helping with homework, encouraging children to read, and promoting school attendance) and school-based activities (such as attending PTA meetings, parent-teacher conferences, concerts, and other school events; helping to raise money for various school-improvement projects; and volunteering at school during the day).

Effects of home environment on learning

Single parent homes

Children with only one parent in the home tend to be somewhat disadvantaged in their educational and subsequent economic success. Children in immigrant families are much less likely than children in native-born families to have only one parent in the home, but there is substantial variation across groups. For example, no more than 10% of children live with one parent among children in immigrant families who have origins in India, Australia and New Zealand, Canada, China, and the Eastern and Southern former Soviet bloc, compared to more than 30% for those with origins in the English-speaking Caribbean, Haiti, and the Dominican Republic. Similarly, the proportion with one parent in the home is 17% to 25% for children in native-born families who are white or Asian, compared to about 50% or more for those who are Central American and mainland-origin Puerto Rican. The variation in number of parents in the household appears to be highly associated with level of parental education. For example, among children in immigrant families, only 10% live with one parent in the high education group, while 17% live with one parent in the medium and low education groups. Among children in native-born families, proportions are 18% for children with high education parents versus 49% for children with low education parents. The number of parents also appears to be highly associated with the age of the children. The proportion with one parent rises from 20% at ages 0-2, to 24% at ages 3-8, and then to 25% at ages 9-13, and 26% at ages 14-17.

Siblings

The presence of brothers and sisters in the home is a mixed blessing for most children. Siblings provide companionship, but they must share available resources. Insofar as parental time and financial resources are limited, parental resources must be spread more thinly in families with a larger number of siblings than in smaller families. Dependent siblings under age 18 are especially likely to compete for parental time and income. As a result, family size can have important consequences for the number of years of school that a child completes, and hence, for economic attainment during adulthood.

Among families of diverse native-born groups, the proportion with four or more siblings in the home ranges from 9% to 11% for Asians, Central Americans, and whites, to 18% for blacks and American Indians. In contrast, among children in immigrant families, the proportion in large families ranges more widely—from a low of 4% to 5% for children with origins in India and China, to a high of 35% for those with origins in the Pacific Islands (other than Australia and New Zealand).

As was the case with the number of parents, the number of siblings in the home also appears to be highly associated with level of parent education. Those children in families with high parental education are least likely to live with four or more siblings.

Grandparents and other relatives

Relatives, such as grandparents and older siblings, and non-relatives in the home can provide childcare or other important resources for children and families, but they may also act as a drain on family resources. Especially in families with few financial resources, doubling-up with other family or non-family members provides a means of sharing scarce resources, and benefiting from economies of scale in paying for housing, energy, food, and other consumable goods. At the same time, doubling-up can also lead to overcrowded housing conditions with negative consequences for children. Taking grandparents, other relatives, and non-relatives together, many children have someone other than a parent or dependent sibling in the home. However, children in newcomer families are nearly twice as likely as those in native-born families to have such a person in the home. Children in white, non-Hispanic native-born or immigrant-origin families are least likely to live with such other persons. About 9% of all children in the United States have at least one grandparent in the home, and whether or not a child lives with a grandparent is strongly correlated with racial/ethnic and immigrant status. For example, living with grandparents is much less common for white children (3%-8%) than for nonwhite children (12%-22%).

Overcrowded home

Overcrowded housing has deleterious effects on child health and well-being, including psychological health and behavioral adjustment, as well as the ability to find a place to do homework undisturbed. Nearly 1 in 5 children live in crowded housing conditions (that is, with more than one person per room). But nearly half of children in immigrant families live in overcrowded housing, compared to only 11% of children in native-born families. There is wide variation among groups, however. Among children in native-born families, the proportion in overcrowded housing ranges from 7% for whites to 40% for Native Hawaiian and other Pacific Islanders. Among children in immigrant families, the proportion in overcrowded housing among white groups is about the same as for native-born white groups, while the highest levels of overcrowding are experienced by children in immigrant families from Central America (59%) and Mexico (67%). Overcrowding is strongly correlated with parental education and poverty across racial/ethnic and immigrant generation groups, suggesting the need to double-up with relatives or non-relatives to share resources. This appears to be especially true among immigrant-origin groups. Moreover, while overcrowding improves slightly for older

versus younger age groups, these reductions tend to be smaller among children in immigrant families, despite their initially higher levels.

Parental education

As families shrank during the last half of the past century, parental education rose. Among adolescents ages 12-17 in 1940, about 70% had parents who had completed no more than 8 years of school, while only 15% had parents who were high school graduates, and 3% had parents who were college graduates. Expenditures for education have expanded enormously since then, and the educational attainment figures have been turned on their head. By 2000, only 6% of adolescents ages 12-17 have parents with no more than 8 years of school, while 82% have parents with high school diplomas, including the 21%-29% who have mothers or fathers with 4-year college degrees.

Parental educational attainment is perhaps the most central feature of family circumstances relevant to overall child well-being and development, regardless of race/ethnicity or immigrant origins. Parents who have completed fewer years of schooling may be less able to help their children with schoolwork because of their limited exposure to knowledge taught in the classroom. They also may be less able to foster their children's educational success in other ways because they lack familiarity with how to negotiate educational institutions successfully. Children whose parents have extremely limited education may, therefore, be more likely to benefit from, or to require, specialized educational program initiatives if their needs are to be met by educational institutions.

Parents with limited educational attainment may also be less familiar with how to access successfully social institutions, such as healthcare, with which children and their parents must interact in

- 60 -

order to receive needed services. Equally important is that parent educational attainment influences their income levels. Parents with limited education tend to command lower wages in the labor market and are, therefore, constrained in the educational, health, and other resources that they can afford to purchase for their children. For all of these reasons, among children generally, negative educational and employment outcomes have been found for children with low parental educational attainment.

Developmental consequences of poverty

In general, poverty has been found to have negative developmental consequences for children. Children in impoverished families may be at risk of educational failure because they lack access to adequate nutrition, health care, dental care, or vision care, as well as lacking access to educational resources that parents with higher incomes can afford to purchase for their children. Children whose parents possess less education have parents who are less able to find full-time year-round work, and the work they find pays less well. As a consequence, policymakers and program administrators in areas with large numbers of children in groups with low parental education tend to have children as clients who not only have parents with limited education, but who work more sporadically, and who have limited income to provide for the needs of their children.

Respectful and reciprocal communication

One simple way to communicate more effectively is to treat the person whom you are addressing respectfully regardless of one's own emotional inclinations. Exhibiting disrespect is almost never helpful, as it immediately places the listener in an adversarial, and probably hostile frame of mind, and encourages them to disregard or dispute anything that is said. This does not mean that one has to agree with everyone and hide any opposition which one may hold to their attitudes, beliefs, values, or positions; it simply means that one should state ones differences in a way that does not belittle another's. For instance, instead of saying "that is a really stupid way of looking at the situation," it is usually more helpful to say "well, I see the situation somewhat differently." Then you can go on to explain how you see it, without ever saying directly that they are "stupid" or even wrong, but simply that it is possible to see things in different ways. Reciprocal communication involves each party receiving equal respect for their ideas and views.

Education law

One function of government is education, which is administered through the public school system by the Federal Department of Education. The states, however, have primary responsibility for the maintenance and operation of public schools. The Federal Government does maintain a heavy interest, however, in education. The National Institute of Education was created to improve education in the United States. Each state is required by its state constitution to provide a school system whereby children may receive an education, and state legislatures exercise power over schools in any manner consistent with the state's constitution. Many state legislatures delegate power over the school system to a state board of education.

Equal Education Opportunities Act of 1974

There is a strong concern for equality in education. Within states this leads to efforts to assure that each child receives an adequate education, no matter where he or she is situated. The Equal Education Opportunities Act of 1974 provides that no state shall deny equal educational opportunity to an individual on the basis of race, color, sex, or national origin.

Title 20- Equal Access

Title 20 states that denial of equal access is prohibited. More precisely:
 (a) Restriction of limited open forum on basis of religious, political, philosophical, or other speech content is prohibited. It shall be unlawful for any public secondary school which receives Federal financial assistance and which has a limited open forum to deny equal access or a fair opportunity to, or discriminate against, any students who wish to conduct a meeting within that limited open forum on the basis of the religious, political, philosophical, or other content of the speech at such meetings.

Confidentiality

Confidentiality provisions help protect families from embarrassing disclosures, discrimination against themselves or their children, differential treatment, and threats to family and job security. Confidentiality provisions also may encourage students or families to take advantage of services designed to help them.
Many of the legal protections to confidentiality are constitutionally based in the fundamental right "to be let alone". Right-to-privacy protections also are reflected in federal and state statutes, statutory privileges, agency regulations, ethical standards and professional practice standards.

FERPA

A 1974 federal law, the Family Educational Rights and Privacy Act (FERPA), protects the privacy interests of students in elementary and secondary schools (and their parents) with regard to certain types of education records. FERPA requires that prior consent be obtained from the student (if 18 or older) or the student's parents before certain types of information can be released from school records. FERPA also gives parents and students access to records, along with the right to challenge the accuracy of those records and make necessary modifications. Changes to FERPA most recently were enacted as part of the Improving Schools Act of 1994, resulting in the issuance of final regulations of FERPA by the U.S. Department of Education. These amendments help promote information sharing by educators.

Inappropriate treatment of students

According to the U.S. Children's Bureau, "More than half (approximately 53%) of all reports alleging maltreatment came from professionals, including educators, law enforcement and justice officials, medical and mental health professionals, social service professionals, and child care providers."

David Finkelhor, Director of the Crimes Against Children Research Center and Codirector of the Family Research Laboratory at the University of New Hampshire says, "The key problem is that educators are confused about what child protection does and whether it does any good." Finkelhor, who has been studying child victimization, child maltreatment, and family violence since 1977, adds, "There is the other problem that schools may not support the reporting process."

Child abuse

Reporting abuse

Teachers are in a unique position to observe and report suspected allegations of child abuse and neglect, but they are in a precarious position for educators - especially neophytes struggling to comprehend various community systems and the vast arena of child abuse reporting laws. Educators should be guided by their school's internal administrative policies for reporting abuse. Sometimes, however, these polices can be confusing. Some schools, for example, encourage educators to report suspected abuse internally before contacting CPS. Nevertheless, state and federal laws mandate educators to report suspected child maltreatment-allowing school administrators to determine if a teacher's suspicions should be reported is unlawful. Because educators are not trained investigators, it is especially important for them to report suspected maltreatment and not assume the responsibility of determining whether a child has been abused.

Reporting child abuse involves a complex array of dynamics. Individual subjectivity, personal perceptions, education, training, and life experiences affect everyone involved in the reporting and investigation process. To maintain objectivity, getting as many facts as possible is essential. Before calling, the reporter should have all of the important information, including the child's name, date of birth, address, telephone number, details of the suspected abuse and information about the suspected perpetrator. Are there bruises or marks? Is the child at risk if he returns home? Callers should be clear about what they are reporting. Vague statements of concern limit the screener's ability when determining whether to assign a case for investigation. Educators need enough information to answer basic questions that will be asked if they call CPS.

When talking to children about suspected abuse, it's imperative not to ask leading questions or insert information. A case can easily become tainted if anyone involved asks leading questions or fills in statements for a child. The incident must be conveyed in the child's own words. Investigators, attorneys, social workers, psychologists, police detectives, and judges will scrutinize statements for information that could appear tainted if a case goes to court.

A recent study published by the American Psychological Association examined how misleading suggestions from parents influenced children's eyewitness reports. Psychologist and coauthor of the study, Debra Ann Poole, says even children as old as 7 or 8 will repeat misinformation. "Apparently," she says, "general instructions to report only what 'really happened' does not always prompt children to make the distinction between events they actually experienced versus events they only heard described by a significant adult."

CAPTA

The federal Child Abuse Prevention and Treatment Act (CAPTA) provides a foundation for states by identifying a minimum set of acts or behaviors that characterize maltreatment. CAPTA also defines what acts are considered physical abuse, neglect, and sexual abuse. Individual states determine and define what warrants further investigation. Civil laws, or statutes, describe the circumstances and conditions that obligate mandated reporters to report known or suspected cases of abuse, with each state providing definitions.

Physical abuse is an intentional injury to a child by the caretaker. It may include but is not limited to burning, beating, kicking, and punching. It is usually the easiest to identify because it often leaves bruises, burns, broken bones, or unexplained injuries. By definition, physical abuse is not accidental, but neither is it necessarily the caretaker's intent to injure the child.

Neglect

Neglect is the most common type of reported and substantiated maltreatment. According to the National Child Abuse and Neglect Data System, of the estimated 826,000 victims of child abuse and neglect in 1999, 58.4% - more than 482,000 children - suffered from neglect; 21.3% were physically abused, and 11.3% were victims of sexual abuse.

Whereas physical abuse tends to be episodic, neglect is more often chronic and involves inattention to a child's basic needs, such as food, clothing, shelter, medical care, and supervision. When considering the possibility of neglect, educators should look for consistencies and ask themselves such questions as:

- Does the child steal or hoard food consistently?
- Does the child consistently demonstrate disorganized thinking or unattended needs?
- Would observing the family in the context of the community provide any answers?
- Is this culturally acceptable child rearing, a different lifestyle, or true neglect?

<u>Sexual abuse</u>

According to CAPTA, sexual abuse is the "employment, use, persuasion, inducement, enticement, or coercion of any child to engage in, or assist any other person to engage in, any sexually explicit conduct or simulation of such conduct for the purpose of producing a visual depiction of such conduct."
Sexual abuse includes any interactions between a child and adult caretaker in which the child is used for the sexual stimulation of the perpetrator or another person. Sexual abuse may also be committed by a person under the age of 18 when that person is either significantly older than the victim or when the perpetrator is in a position of power or control over the child

No Child Left Behind Act

<u>State assessments</u>

This refers to the tests developed by your state that your child will take every year in grades 3-8 and at least once in high school. Using these tests, the state will be able to compare schools to each other and know which ones need extra help to improve.

Parents can contact your child's school or school district to find out more details about your state's tests.

<u>AYP</u>

Adequate Yearly Progress (AYP) is the term which the No Child Left Behind Act uses to explain that a child's school has met state reading and math goals. Your school district's report card will let you know whether or not your child's school has made AYP.

<u>School in need of improvement</u>

This is the term No Child Left Behind uses to refer to schools receiving Title I funds that have not met state reading and math goals (AYP) for at least two years. If a child's school is labeled a "school in need of improvement," it receives extra help to improve and the child has the option to transfer to another public school, including a public charter school. Also, your child may be eligible to receive free tutoring and extra help with schoolwork. Contact your child's school district to find out if your child qualifies.

<u>SES</u>

Supplemental Educational Services (SES) is the term which the No Child Left Behind Act uses to refer to the tutoring and extra help with schoolwork in subjects such as reading and math that children from low-income families may be eligible to receive. This help is provided free of charge and generally takes place outside the regular school day, such as after school or during the summer.

<u>HQT</u>

Highly Qualified Teacher (HQT) is the term which the No Child Left Behind Act uses for a teacher who proves that he or she knows the subjects he or she is teaching, has a college degree, and is state-certified. No Child Left Behind requires that a child be taught by a Highly Qualified Teacher in core academic subjects.

Special education teachers

Special education teachers work with children and youths who have a variety of disabilities. A small number of special education teachers work with students with intellectual disabilities or autism, primarily teaching them life skills and basic literacy. However, the majority of special education teachers work with children with mild to moderate disabilities, using the general education curriculum, or modifying it, to meet the child's individual needs. Most special education teachers instruct students at the elementary, middle, and secondary school level, although some teachers work with infants and toddlers.

Practice Test

Practice Questions

1. Which statement is false?
   a. Before creating lesson plans, a teacher should analyze the curriculum and educational goals of the course being taught.
   b. Students often benefit from knowing the intended learning objectives as well as time frames for instruction ahead of time.
   c. Teachers should refrain from sharing information about learning goals with students so that they can make their own assumptions and connections.
   d. Lesson plans should be flexible so that teachers and students can explore areas of spontaneous interest during class time.

2. Which of the following choices is the best use of homework in regular instruction?
   a. A daily review of classroom concepts to keep information fresh for the next day's lessons.
   b. A weekly packet that includes both review of concepts as well as opportunities to practice transferring the skills to new situations.
   c. Monthly "extension" projects that require students to research and apply skills to topics of their own choosing.
   d. Homework should not be used as a major part of instruction, since teachers cannot be present to guide students.

3. What must a teacher do before he or she will be able to evaluate the effectiveness of the instructional design?
   a. Create an outline of class objectives and how each objective will be assessed or measured.
   b. Interpret and analyze student performance on each assignment.
   c. Request assistance from peers in observing class instruction and giving vital feedback.
   d. Determine each student's capacity for learning.

4. How can a teacher evaluate student mastery of intended learning outcomes over time?
   a. Analyzing classroom and standardized test scores throughout the year.
   b. Gauging student understanding during classroom discussion and group projects.
   c. Through a combination of student class work, presentations, performance on assignments, test scores, and participation during class time.
   d. Meeting with each student on a monthly basis to discuss classroom concepts, allowing the teacher to assess whether or not each one can demonstrate mastery.

5. A history teacher and language teacher work together in creating units of instruction. The history teacher presents lessons that introduce historical events and changes in culture. The language teacher introduces literary texts created during the period of time being studied in history class. What is their most likely intention in designing instruction?

    a. To simplify the planning process by sharing resources and techniques, thus leaving more time for discussion and application.

    b. To allow students to activate prior knowledge and make conceptual connections between the two contexts.

    c. To show that art is usually rooted in the culture of the creator.

    d. To reinforce that some subjects are more interconnected than others and contain mutually important concepts.

6. Which answer describes the best example of an introductory lesson on the concept of generalization?

    a. Mr. Smith asks each of his students to write down one idea, fact, opinion, or belief onto a note card and turn it in. The class then plays a game in which the students are a "jury." Mr. Smith reads the note cards aloud one at a time and the class must vote on which statements are general and which ones are specific.

    b. Mrs. Cameron provides each student with a common classroom or household object. The students sort themselves into groups based on how the objects are similar. Finally, each group will choose a name based on their object theme and explain it to the class.

    c. Ms. Jereaux reviews each text her students have read in language class during the past month. She asks the students how the texts are alike or unalike and asks them to explain their answers. The class creates general and specific statements together.

    d. Ms. Thomas presents a graphic organizer with two columns: one column is dedicated to "general" ideas and the other to "specific" ideas. As the students participate in their science lab experiment, they record their observations into the appropriate columns.

7. A teacher with a combined classroom of 1st- and 2nd-graders utilizes integrated language instruction. Each time she presents a new word list to her students, those words are used in vocabulary, spelling, grammar, reading and writing work. What is the benefit of this type of instruction?

    a. The students learn the words thoroughly by using them in a variety of contexts.

    b. The teacher makes instruction and learning more streamlined by re-using the same words in each lesson.

    c. The teacher can identify the areas of language the students need most help with by controlling the number and types of words presented.

    d. The students learn that all concepts are truly integrated and that no idea stands alone.

8. A new Social Studies teacher is looking through a large curriculum binder supplied by her school district. Each concept is detailed extensively and the teachers are expected to present each one in sequential order. How can the teacher inspire students to become interested in and responsible for learning the material?

    a. By rewarding the students after each instruction unit with a fun activity, such as a movie, favorite game, or free discussion day.

    b. By regularly encouraging students to discuss how the lesson material relates to their everyday lives and experiences.

    c. By organizing the curriculum into general content clusters and providing students with outlines so that they understand the intended learning outcomes.

    d. By introducing weekly projects and exercises that provide variety, such as performing skits, comparing historical and current events, or holding mock debates.

9. Which quote is the best example of a clear and measurable curriculum objective?

    a. "By the end of the course, students will understand the publishing process."

    b. "Each student will significantly improve computation skills."

    c. "Each student will demonstrate understanding of the Scientific Method by completing an independent science project."

    d. "All students will learn to transfer knowledge between contexts via comparisons and discussions."

Use the information below to answer questions 10-11.

    An art teacher starts the school term by asking his students to brainstorm. He writes "Art _____" and asks the students to "fill in the blank" with their own ideas and beliefs about the subject. After class, the teacher picks the contributions that describe his teaching objectives for the term and posts each one onto large individual felt boards around his classroom. The remaining entries will be used as part of a collage-making exercise later in the term.

10. Which choice is the best way to complete this exercise so that students internalize the objectives for the course, both in concept and application?

    a. The teacher can identify student pieces that reflect the learning objectives on the felt boards and ask students to post their work over the course of the term.

    b. Introduce a second brainstorm halfway through the term to determine whether or not student perceptions remain the same.

    c. Ask students to review the ideas on each felt board on a weekly basis to assist them with retaining the information.

    d. Require students to write word and phrases that relate to each idea and post them on the felt boards at regular intervals.

11. What is the teacher's most likely intention behind this method?

    a. To inspire independent thinking among students

    b. To engage the student's linguistic and intellectual participation in addition to creative pursuits

    c. To help students organize and internalize the major concepts they are expected to learn throughout the course

    d. To monitor student perceptions over time

12. Which lesson uses the chunking strategy to help students understand and retain information?
    a. The teacher leads the class in reviewing requirements for the year-end project, including topic choices, project components, and grading procedures.
    b. The class is sorted into small groups to complete assignments, based on the notion that group dynamics will support communication and expression of ideas.
    c. A math teacher reviews the principles of multiplication prior to introducing division.
    d. A science teacher shows students how to take notes by drawing a line down the center of a piece of paper and writing major concepts to the left and details or supporting information to the right.

13. Which statement is true?
    a. An important part of teaching is showing students ways to transfer information from their limited, short-term (working) memories to their long-term memories.
    b. Memorization is the key technique in improving student retention of information.
    c. Teachers should always try to create new ways of helping students retrieve information that is buried in sensory memory.
    d. Memory always improves when students are taught from "the bottom up," meaning that they learn specific facts first, and later learn to apply those facts to larger, broader concepts.

14. Which skill or set of skills should be consistently reviewed over time?
    a. Mastered concepts that are not used in subsequent lessons or operations within the classroom.
    b. Mastered concepts that are used in subsequent lessons or operations within the classroom.
    c. Previews of lessons and concepts that are going to be introduced later in the course.
    d. All details and examples used to illustrate the broader curricular points in each class period.

15. Which graphic organizer would be most helpful for practice with comparison and contrasting of ideas or objects?
    a. SQ3R chart
    b. Venn diagram
    c. Flower diagram for the "5 W's"
    d. Bar graph

16. Mr. Payne is working with a group of students for whom English is not a first language. His students understand the concept of cause and effect relationships, but are having trouble recognizing examples within a given text. Which approach is most appropriate?
    a. Consistently review as many examples as possible to assist with skill transfer to the given text.
    b. Teach students how to identify and interpret important linking words such as because, due to, leading to, inasmuch, since.
    c. Demonstrate identifying the order of events and explain that the first event mentioned in the text is typically the cause.
    d. Demonstrate how to isolate each sentence and divide into separate components based on cause and effect events.

17. Which theory would most support the following statement? There are many 'ways of knowing,' all equal to one another: each student will learn in his or her own manner.
    a. Bloom's taxonomy
    b. Situated learning
    c. Problem-based learning
    d. Multiple intelligences

18. Which of the following choices would not directly support reading comprehension in new material?
    a. Providing a text outline for the material with space for note-taking
    b. Discussing important upcoming concepts in the text
    c. Asking for student opinions and beliefs about content in the material
    d. Demonstrating the process of "actively skimming" the text before reading in-depth

19. Ms. Hanks is ready to introduce a new unit on grammar. In her experience, students do not enjoy this subject and tend to have a negative attitude about the lessons. Which approach will help her solve this potential problem?
    a. Perform a teacher-composed rap or song about grammar to get the students interested in the lessons.
    b. Incorporate activities into the lessons: mnemonics and songs for memory, computer games for practice, and drawing exercises to demonstrate relationships among parts of speech and language.
    c. Invite speakers from various professions to speak to the students about how they use knowledge of grammar every day, showing the importance of learning the material at a young age.
    d. Discuss the importance of grammar with the students and reward them with treats of their choosing for participation and effort.

Use the following graphic to answer questions 20 and 21.

Directions: Record your ideas in the appropriate boxes.

What I Know	What I Want to Know	What I Learned

20. A teacher provides her students with the above graphic before class. What technique is she planning to introduce?
    a. KWL
    b. The 3 W's
    c. Active Learning Matrix
    d. KKL

21. Which learning outcome is most likely intended?
    a. Comprehensive review for test-taking
    b. Pre-writing practice
    c. Self-monitoring lesson or reading comprehension
    d. Basic model for scientific experiments

22. A high-school chemistry teacher is preparing her lesson plans for the next month. The upcoming unit includes a large amount of complex math that will serve as the foundation for future units. Which daily lesson structure is most appropriate?

a. Teacher-led review of previous day's content, short demonstration/instruction of concepts, break, group practice, students present results of practice and discuss as a class

b. Video tutorial, short demonstration/instruction of concepts, student-led review of concepts, complete homework for the upcoming evening in-class

c. Fun group activity involving movement, teacher-led demonstration/instruction of concepts in detailed format, working each problem in a step-by-step manner, student questions

d. Short lecture on purpose of class instruction, short teacher-led demonstration/instruction, students take turns working examples in front of the class

23. Which method is best for connecting students' personal experiences to course concepts?

a. Each time a new concept is introduced in Social Studies class, students take turns relating a personal anecdote that exemplifies the material.

b. Keep a running list in Algebra class of how concepts are used in various professions.

c. For a year-end Science project, students pick a topic to research. The written report must include a section describing why the topic is of personal importance to the student.

d. In Psychology class, require weekly journal entries in which students draw or write about personal reflections, provided that entries reflect on concepts taught during the week.

24. A teacher of elementary-aged students will begin to incorporate pop quizzes into her weekly lessons. During the quizzes, students will answer questions based on previous lessons and homework assignments. What is the best way to approach this new activity?

a. Talk about the quizzes for one to two days before delivering them, taking care to explain that their purpose is to check retention of information and ensure that homework is being completed.

b. Surprise the students with the activity, modeling excitement and interest in doing something new.

c. Provide the students with the quizzes and instruct them to work quickly and quietly, but do not tell them they are being graded.

d. Talk about the importance of great performance on assignments and describe how taking the quizzes will prepare students for upcoming high-stakes testing.

25. Which approach is best for beginning to teach a group of new students?

a. Rely on age- and grade-appropriate standards to determine the starting point in the curriculum.

b. Review samples of past class work or test scores, if available, in conjunction with teacher-administered assessment to determine a starting point.

c. Talk with students to gauge their intellectual and maturity levels and attempt to "jump-start" them by introducing challenging work immediately.

d. Ask students to list their interests in detail and use the lists to design instruction that will maintain their attention throughout the course.

26. Which statement is false?
    a. Class material should be presented in a logical sequence based on the objectives of the course.
    b. Sequence of lessons can have a variety of foundations: time frames, progression of ideas, overview of topics, or building of skills.
    c. All components of a lesson sequence must be presented in detail, even if all students have previously demonstrated comprehension.
    d. Instruction sequencing can often be shared with students to facilitate understanding.

27. Which material should first be taught in small steps over the course of several weeks?
    a. Long division
    b. Writing a research paper
    c. Concepts of melody and harmony
    d. Long-term effects of the American Revolution

Use the information below to answer questions 28 and 29.

   Each year, middle-school students score poorly on the Problem Solving portion of their standardized tests. These scores reflect problem-solving abilities across a wide range of subjects. Teachers are given the responsibility of preparing the students to use these skills in daily life as well as on the tests.

28. Which approach should not be included in the teachers' plan?
    a. Weekly activities in which students are given real examples of problems and asked to work with a group to provide a solution
    b. Teacher-led instruction on problem-solving frameworks
    c. Students suggest problems from personal experience to be discussed and solved by the class
    d. Model erroneous, ill-conceived, or vague problem-solving methods and ways to correct them

29. In addition to standardized test scores, how should students' progress be measured?
    a. Percentage of correct answers on all problems presented in class or for homework
    b. Running record of teacher observations during class problem-solving exercises
    c. Graded individual assignments in which students solve problems and provide explanations of solutions were reached
    d. Group demonstrations of real-life problem-solving techniques

30. Which scenario describes the most effective use of vocabulary practice or instruction on new words?
    a. Each new word is written three to five times in neat handwriting, defined in the student's own words, and written in an original sentence.
    b. When reading together in Social Studies, the teacher will pause to allow students to highlight and underline important vocabulary words in their textbooks. The class discusses the word meanings together.
    c. Students have computer time during which they play vocabulary and other language games, both learning new words and reviewing previously-taught words.
    d. Students work together to define new words from previous knowledge or reference sources. The class divides into teams to play charades. Each student is given a vocabulary word and must "enact" the word's meaning for his or her team.

Use the information below to answer questions 31 and 32.

Ms. Shomari teaches math for students in 3rd, 4th and 5th grades. She typically uses the CRA approach with her students to ensure that they understand each concept fully.

CRA

C	Concrete phase	Model or demonstrate concepts using tangible materials
R	Representational phase	Introduce representations of tangible materials to practice concepts
A	Abstract phase	Use abstract symbols and words to practice concepts

31. Which lesson is given during the representational phase?
    a. Students practice multiplication facts by bouncing a ball or jack between hearing the question and providing the answers.
    b. Each student is given a worksheet with addition and subtraction problems to complete during a timed drill.
    c. The teacher shows students how to multiply by using groups of beads, jacks or other objects.
    d. The teacher shows students a workbook in which students answer multiplication problems using pictures of beads, jacks or other objects.

32. Which choice would not indicate that a student is ready to practice a concept in the abstract phase?
    a. After the initial concrete lesson, the student is able to repeat the explanation and/or demonstration during review.
    b. The student demonstrates the concept in his or her work without using representational materials.
    c. During lesson time, a student suggests to her teacher that using the beads or pictures of beads is "the same thing" as the math facts listed on a poster in the classroom.
    d. The student asks to practice concepts abstractly, saying he does not need the materials or representations any longer.

33. Aside from test scores, how might a teacher identify patterned gaps in student knowledge or understanding throughout instruction?
    a. Student responses during in-class, verbal comprehension checks
    b. Student engagement and participation during class and group projects
    c. Both A and B
    d. Neither A nor B

34. Which teaching technique is described by the following statements?   The teacher provides motivation, context, and modeling when presenting subject material. Slowly, the teacher reduces guidance and interaction so that the student can become independent with the material.
    a. Metacognition
    b. Scaffolding
    c. Bradley method
    d. SWT

35. Which answer describes the best use of concept extensions in the classroom?
   a. During the course of the year, each student in Biology class is permitted to choose a topic of interest and research it. The research is then presented to the class with visual and/or media aids.
   b. Whenever a student comes across a word that he does not understand, his teacher shows him how to use context clues or reference sources to find its meaning.
   c. Each week during a unit on biodiversity, students visit the lake besides their school to observe and record information about plant and animals living there. Each entry must be accompanied by class reading and lecture notes.
   d. A Social Sciences teacher instructs her students to interview one person over the age of 65 for a final project. The students prepare a written report and participate in a classroom discussion about what they learned.

36. Which statement is false?
   a. Metaphors and analogies are often useful in learning new concepts through activation of prior knowledge.
   b. Metaphors and analogies compare things that are not the same, but that have some similarities.
   c. Analogies should be presented before metaphorical concepts, since the former concept is more specific and is easier for students to grasp.
   d. None of the above

37. The upcoming Social Studies test will cover civics concepts. Much of the content is abstract in nature. How can the teacher understand whether or not the students have truly mastered the concepts?
   a. Create a multiple-choice and fill-in-the-blank test that simplifies the content and makes it clear and easy for students to understand.
   b. Include a section that lists main thematic elements and asks students to explain each concept in their own words.
   c. Allow students to work cooperatively in small groups to answer test questions.
   d. Allow students to use their notes and books to answer test questions.

38. Which choice describes the most effective instructional design for the corresponding activity?
   a. Students are placed into groups of three to work together on the first chemistry experiment of the year. They record findings on a log sheet created by the teacher.
   b. Each student is given ten minutes at the end of class time to review important concepts independently.
   c. Given that a few students performed poorly on the last unit test, the next day's lessons are devoted to reviewing the concepts as a class.
   d. Following a written comprehension quiz, the teacher instructs students to switch papers with a partner to grade them quickly; each student then has time to correct his or her own work before turning it in.

39. Which technique would likely facilitate more effective small-group activities?
   a. When assigning groups, take great care not to place students who are close friends or who do not get along well into the same group.
   b. Part of the assignment is to determine group member "roles" so that all group members are aware of their own and others' responsibilities.
   c. Keep students assigned to the same group throughout the course unless there are significant problems to establish continuity and development of cooperation.
   d. Change group assignments for each activity to facilitate growth and variation in cooperative learning.

40. Which set of circumstances provides the best opportunity for enhancing learning with appropriate questioning techniques?
   a. Students' appear to be confused about what the teacher is saying.
   b. Students are slowly becoming disengaged from class instruction and have begun doodling, passing notes or daydreaming.
   c. Students appear to have a good understanding of the factual lesson content but have not yet learned how to apply it.
   d. All of the above

41. A student asks a question in class that the teacher feels should already have been answered during class lecture and discussion. How should he respond?
   a. Remind the student that this information has already been covered and that he should try and increase his attention level.
   b. Direct the student to the place in the text book where the answer can be found.
   c. Open the question to the class and ask if there is another student who can provide the answer.
   d. Answer his question as quickly as possible and continue the lecture.

42. Which choice is not an effective questioning technique?
   a. Asking more than one question at once so that the student can choose which one he or she feels more comfortable answering
   b. Phrasing a specific and direct question to reduce confusion
   c. Providing a wait time of at least three to five seconds to give the student time to think and construct an answer
   d. Acknowledge and encourage effort in attempting to answer the question even if the response is incorrect

43. Ms. Bloom's students rarely ask questions in class. She wants to make sure she is addressing any questions they may have and that they are thinking critically enough about the material to create opportunities for further learning. How can she accomplish her goals?
   a. Require each student to be ready to ask one question per week and keep track of the content, structure and frequency of each student's contributions.
   b. Use a weekly think-pair-share activity in which students create and answer questions in small groups.
   c. Instruct students to write questions related to class content as part of their homework and choose a new set each week to present theirs to the class for discussion.
   d. Stop instruction periodically to ask if there are any questions. Maintain an intentional silence during this time to give students time to think about their questions and encourage participation.

44. Which type of question would be most likely to develop higher-level, abstract thinking skills in students?
    a. Convergent
    b. Closed
    c. Clarifying
    d. Elaborating

45. Research suggests that a students' attention span wanes throughout class. Which lesson structure will promote the greatest level of comprehension, growth, and retention of concepts?
    a. Socratic question and answer format
    b. Lecture and review
    c. Activity-based, hands-on engagement
    d. Alternating between direct instruction and group/independent activities

46. Which classroom arrangement is most appropriate for young students in Kindergarten or 1st grade?
    a. Child-sized desks and chairs are placed in a neat grid so that the teacher can always see whether or not the students are in place and on task. All personal belongings, supplies and class work are kept inside individual desk cubbies.
    b. Lamps, rugs, and cozy pillows create a home-like atmosphere. Artwork and 'found' objects decorate the halls and tables. When group lessons are given, the students simply listen from wherever they are in the classroom.
    c. Certain curriculum areas each have a designated classroom space. Seating is provided in each area and is designed to match the nature of the activities present. Whole-class seating is available at long, arced tables in one area of the room.
    d. The classroom chairs and desks are arranged in a U shape to promote discussion and collaboration among students. The children alternate between desks and outdoor play.

47. Which classroom arrangement is most appropriate for a high school Civics class?
    a. Desks and chairs are arranged into rows. Posters are hung on the walls outlining fundamental important classroom concepts. All chairs face the front of the room, where the teacher lectures.
    b. The arrangement changes based on the type of class structure for the week. For lectures and class discussion, students sit in a circle. For small group work, students sit in small groups. At times, the floor may be cleared for activities or audiovisual displays.
    c. Students sit on comfortable chairs and couches during class. The teacher moves around the room to engage the students in lecture, discussion, or activities.
    d. The class is arranged into learning stations. Students move through the stations during self-directed class time and are able to work with partners if they so choose.

48. Middle school classes will soon be studying poetry for a month. Which homework assignment(s) will support the lessons most effectively?

    a. Each student will choose a poet from a teacher-provided list and compose a short report on his or her life. During the unit, each student will either present a poem written by the poet in a creative way or write an original poem in the same style.

    b. Each student receives a graphic organizer to work on at home. Students must fill in the organizer with types of poetry and their functions. In class, students will correct any homework mistakes and use the work to study for the test.

    c. Each student must write a number of original poems. Writing can cover any chosen type of poem. The number of poems written is determined by the grade level of the student.

    d. Each student will memorize a famous poem selected from a list. The poems will be recited during a classroom Poetry Slam, to which other classes will be invited. Students will dress up and provide refreshments to the audience.

49. Which choice is the best use of the rehearsal method in class?

    a. Before presenting to the class, student groups practice their group presentations fully.

    b. Students learn and sing songs to help them remember detailed concepts such as state names, the alphabet, or a sequence of steps.

    c. Each day before class, the teacher leads students in reciting the overall class objectives to help internalize relationships between major ideas and daily lessons.

    d. Students break into groups to practice and drill concepts for the upcoming test.

50. Which choice is not an effective way to reduce performance anxiety in school?

    a. Create a variety of formats and settings for assessments or assignments.

    b. Build relationships with students and know what interests and motivates them.

    c. Counsel students in the event of "failure," identifying ways to improve performance next time.

    d. Frequently discuss school experiences and how what students do now affects their opportunities later. Emphasize effort and engagement over performance markers.

51. Which statement is most true regarding classroom rules?

    a. Students are most likely to internalize and take responsibility for following rules when they can be involved in creating them.

    b. Teachers should make classroom rule lists as detailed and expansive as possible to cover all situations and eliminate any room for confusion.

    c. The most important rule in any classroom is based on the concept: When you are unsure of what to do, always ask the teacher before proceeding.

    d. Classroom rules should be modified over time to fit the students, scenarios, and needs in the specific class.

52. One of Mr. Croft's rules is that students always turn in their neatest, best personal work. Holly breaks this rule when she turns in homework that is sloppily prepared and mostly incorrect. Mr. Croft is surprised since her work is almost always of high quality, or at the least is reflective of more effort. What is the best response in this situation?

    a. Express disappointment in Holly's lack of effort and give her the grade that matches the quality of her work.

    b. Interpret Holly's work as an indication that concepts need to be re-taught in class.

    c. Ask Holly to re-do the homework to the best of her ability and allow her to achieve up to 80% of the maximum points for the assignment.

    d. Both B and C

53. Which strategy is most effective for managing an elementary classroom's duties (e.g. line leaders, lunch helpers, hall monitors, sharpening pencils, light classroom cleaning)?
   a. Give each student in the classroom a job such as sharpening pencils or leading the line and rotate job assignments once a month.
   b. Demonstrate that only students who show exceptional behavior and work habits will be chosen for certain classroom duties.
   c. Demonstrate that only students who show negative behavior and work habits will be chosen for certain classroom duties.
   d. Allow students to choose their duties in the classroom.

54. Which classroom routine would most likely result in a calm, productive and orderly start to the school day?
   a. When students arrive, they have a half-hour of free time during which to put belongings away, socialize, use the restroom, or finish up homework.
   b. The first assignment of the day is written on the large whiteboard in front of the class. Students are expected to get settled and begin working quietly while the teacher prepares for lessons.
   c. The agenda for the day is written on the large whiteboard in front of class before school starts and all needed materials are accessible. The teacher stands at the door to greet each student and re-direct those who are off-task.
   d. Each morning begins with a new and fun activity, such as a scavenger hunt, mystery game, or social time. The first student to arrive is told what to do and then students work cooperatively on arrival to share and complete the tasks.

55. When would it be prudent for a teacher to halt a class discussion topic and offer to talk with the involved students outside of class time?
   a. Whenever students disagree about an issue that has multiple facets and solutions
   b. When he or she senses that the entire class is not interested or engaged in the topic being discussed
   c. The topic at hand could be uncomfortable for some students to discuss.
   d. The tone of discussion becomes too personal or feels like an attack

56. Which response is most effective in building a young student's intrinsic self-confidence?
   a. "I am so proud of your grade on this test! You have really improved in your test-taking skills this term."
   b. "You completed your project! You did it! I know it was difficult for you at first—how do you feel about the project now?"
   c. "This is the type of work I expect from you each day. Now that we both see what you are capable of, I will look forward to seeing you shine on all your assignments!"
   d. "The only person who can tell you what to do in this situation is you. You should have confidence in yourself that you can solve this problem without my help."

57. A young boy in the 1st grade is struggling to stay on task and keep his body under control during class. His constant movements are distracting other students and keeping him from completing the day's work. How should the situation be handled in the classroom?

a. Sit with him and break down the day's work into smaller segments. Help him alternate between physical activities just outside the classroom (such as jumping jacks or running errands in the hallway) and completing his segmented activities for the day.

b. Agree upon a non-verbal signal. When the signal (clearing the throat, touching the nose) is given, the boy is reminded to sit down and focus on his work.

c. Call his name sharply in class to get his attention. Clearly communicate the expectations for behavior and work completion so that he knows what he should be doing.

d. Call his parents to discuss the problem. Suggest having him evaluated for certain learning difficulties so that all adults involved in his care can work together to help him.

58. Mira, a 9th-grade student, is falling behind this term. She spends much of her class time daydreaming or doodling in her notebook. Mira also talks excessively to friends during independent work time. How should her teacher respond?

a. Call Mira's parents to arrange a meeting and discuss what might be going on at home that is affecting her class performance.

b. No action is necessary; some students will enjoy certain classes more than others and should not be expected to participate at their highest potential in every situation.

c. Communicate the consequences of her actions very clearly, so that Mira knows what will happen if her negative behavior continues.

d. Discuss the problem with Mira outside of class to determine why she is not engaged. Agree upon a plan of action together.

59. Which statement is true regarding classroom comportment and behavior?

a. By the time each child reaches school-age, he or she knows how to behave well. Teachers should expect good behavior at all times and enforce clearly-defined rules; children respond positively to high expectations.

b. Young people are still learning how to behave in desired ways throughout their early years. Teachers should vary interventions for undesired behaviors and establish clear and logical consequences for students' actions.

c. When a student is making bad choices, it is often effective to address the student in the presence of his or her peers for accountability's sake. A bit of embarrassment will help the student correct misbehavior more quickly.

d. Misbehavior is a sign of deeper problems in class or at home. Teachers should intervene immediately and partner with parents to ensure that students get the help they need.

60. In which scenario would non-verbal communication be most effective in correcting misbehavior?

a. During group time, Harry and Nina have gotten off-task and are chatting and giggling.

b. Allison has failed to return her homework for the third week in a row.

c. Haley has climbed an unstable tree on school grounds.

d. Class discussion has become heated and John is asserting his position by making verbal attacks on other students.

Use the information below to answer questions 61 and 62.

Mrs. Norris has become increasingly frustrated with her 8th-grade class. Despite her best intentions, the students continue to waste class time by talking excessively during transitions and not listening to instructions. She has also noticed that the students seem to argue more frequently, resulting in lingering negativity amongst class mates. As a result of these problems, Mrs. Norris has fallen behind in her instructional plans and some students are struggling with various assignments and concepts. She considers the following actions to correct the classroom issues:

A.	Do nothing; this behavior is normal at this age. Encourage better behavior on an ongoing basis.	F.	Suspend any instigating students from class activities.
B.	Allow students to experience the natural consequences of their actions (i.e. lower grades, frustration).	G.	Set and revisit clear consequences for undesired behaviors.
C.	Hold a class meeting to identify the reasons for and results of the observed behaviors.	H.	Communicate high expectations for students' ability to correct the problems.
D.	Communicate frustration and anger and the results of students' behavior.	I.	Teach and model conflict-resolution and problem-solving skills on an ongoing basis.
E.	Speak only to the specific students involved in problematic behaviors; do not force those behaving well to work through irrelevant issues.	J.	Ask a respected male teacher to speak to the students about their actions.

61. Which set of responses would constitute the best initial approach for Mrs. Norris to take?
    a. A and B
    b. B, D, F and J
    c. B, E, H, and I
    d. C, G, H and I

62. How should Mrs. Norris respond if and when the classroom issues begin to improve?
    a. Ask the students to write journal entries about their perceptions of the resolution.
    b. Allow the students to realize for themselves how they are benefitting from the changes in class.
    c. Discuss the changes on an ongoing basis in class to help students identify feelings about the changes in class.
    d. Speak to the specific students involved in the conflicts to discuss improvements and feelings.

63. Which time-out strategy is most effective for very young students?
    a. None; time-out has been proven ineffective for young students.
    b. Warn the student of the consequences before delivering it; make him sit silently and alone for a set amount of time; warn him that repeated offenses will result in the same consequence; allow him to rejoin activity.
    c. Make the student sit away from the group, ideally facing away from activity, and then require the child to apologize for her actions before rejoining the group; failure to apologize results in longer time spent away from the group.
    d. Warn the student of the consequence; if action is repeated, make him sit away from the group for a set amount of time; debrief with student about the reasons for the time out; communicate expectation for behavior before rejoining activity.

64. A high-school class is holding a review for their upcoming history test. They have a large amount of information to cover in one class period. How should their teacher respond to correct answers?

a. Organize a mock "academic bowl" by grouping students into teams. The teacher keeps track of correct answers and rewards the winning team with something sweet.

b. Follow the format of the test in asking questions and indicate which responses should be recorded for future study.

c. Toss out a piece of candy to each student who provides a correct answer.

d. Smile and verbally praise students when they provide correct answers.

65. Students have been enacting a play in class for the past several days. Following its completion, the teacher wants to begin discussion. His first discussion question involves analysis of the play's themes and is met by silence and stares from students. What should he do?

a. Break the question down into a simpler, shorter format to get discussion moving, and then build up to more complex questions.

b. Wait quietly until someone offers an answer.

c. Call on one of the brighter students in class and ask her try and answer the question as best she can.

d. Tell the students that they must have failed to pay attention to the storyline if this particular question is too difficult for them.

66. Which of the following choices is the best description of using homework as an educational tool for older students?

a. Algebra equations listed in the student textbook that provide practice similar to the day's class instruction.

b. Chapters to be covered during class lecture are assigned for home reading at least one week in advance.

c. Student/Parent chart used to record time spent each night practicing spelling words for the week; completed charts are turned in for rewards before test time.

d. Monthly packets that include some preview and review readings, practice with examples, as well as two short experiments that will test students' application skills.

67. Based on information provided in Question 66, how might a teacher respond to returned homework to facilitate student learning?

a. Go over the homework in class, asking students if they have any questions on the practice equations. Provide correct answers so students can correct their work.

b. Ensure that class lectures follow the information presented in assigned text readings. Occasionally administer pop quizzes over the reading to determine whether or not students are completing homework and have understood what they read.

c. Give a weekly homework grade for completion of spelling practice in order to motivate parents and students to practice together. Homework grades count for 10% of the student's overall grade in class.

d. Have students turn in a homework journal, within which each student records observations, thoughts, and results of each homework assignment. The teacher provides guidelines for acceptable journal entries and provides grades accordingly.

68. Select the answer that most truthfully completes the following statement. Classroom rewards and recognition…

a. should be delivered in frequent but unpredictable patterns so that students are always striving to earn them.

b. should be based on things students can control, such as attitude, effort, or improvement.

c. must be explained in detailed way before each assignment or task so that students know what they are working toward at all times.

d. are often damaging to student morale, especially when individuals do not receive anticipated praise or rewards.

69. What type of incentive would be most appropriate for talkative students who are inconsistent in finishing their class work?

a. Reduce the amount of work required for these students so that they can feel successful at first.

b. Provide candy or treats for each assignment finished.

c. Once the daily class work is complete, students are permitted to choose between outdoor recess and indoor social time.

d. If class work is completed for the day, students are given a chance to start on their homework early, possibly eliminating the need to take work home at the end of the day.

70. Which use of punishment or consequences is most effective?

a. Adrian was disruptive and not respectful during class lessons and group work despite repeated requests from the teacher to change his behavior. Adrian has to stay after school and clean the blackboards, sharpen pencils, and complete other classroom tasks.

b. Tamyra is extremely fidgety and cannot sit still during class. Sometimes, she distracts other students. Tamyra's teacher moves her desk into a space at the back of the class, away from the other students.

c. Barron is caught skipping class. He receives one day of school suspension. Administrators warn him that if he skips class again, he will be suspended for a longer period of time and possibly expelled from school.

d. Linda and Ellie are found to have cheated on their science quiz by working together when the teacher was not watching. They each would have made an 88%, but their teacher decides to give them each one-half that grade, resulting in a 44%. They must each sit alone during individual work for the remainder of the term.

71. Tyler is a very popular and well-liked sophomore in Ms. Eden's language arts class. Ms. Eden appreciates Tyler's willingness to participate in class discussion, but has noticed that his answers are usually incorrect or off-topic. How should she respond?

  a. Speak to Tyler after class and explain the problem to him. Express concern over his pattern of incorrect responses and suggest that he find a study partner or tutor to help him prepare more effectively for class.

  b. Initiate a one-response rule for class discussion so that Tyler cannot offer multiple answers in class. Other students will have more opportunities to answer and Tyler will suffer less embarrassment in front of his peers.

  c. Talk to all the students about the purpose of class discussions, namely, that students should share ideas that are supported by class lessons and independent learning. Require students to provide at least one piece of textual evidence and/or an explanation of their thought process for each answer they give during discussion.

  d. Use humor to address the issue during class. Start a tally chart on the chalkboard for Tyler's incorrect answers. Involve his classmates in gentle teasing about his habit and give Tyler a mock reward when he reaches a pre-determined number of tally marks on the chart.

72. When is it appropriate for a teacher to lower his or her expectation of a student or group of students?

  a. Never. Teachers who hold consistently high expectations for student achievement usually see better results than those who do not.

  b. When the vast majority of the group has demonstrated effort but has either missed the point of an assignment or failed to complete it successfully.

  c. When he or she is teaching students who are disabled or extremely disadvantaged compared to the rest of the group.

  d. Teachers should not operate based on expectations; students are all different and must learn in highly personal ways. The learning process should be a shared discovery, rather than establishing and meeting of expectations.

Use the information below to answer questions 73 and 74.

  Ms. Baird's class will be completing an in-depth project over the course of the next 18 weeks. Students will work on the projects both inside and outside of class. The projects must all be related to classroom instruction on ancient civilizations, but students may pick their specific topics. All projects will include research, written components, oral presentation, and creative construction of models and visual aids.

73. Which appendix or appendices should be provided when Mrs. Baird introduces the project requirements to the class?

  a. Letter to parents describing the project assignment, components, due dates, and other pertinent information

  b. Checklist of components

  c. Rubric describing each component and descriptions of student performance at each grading level

  d. Examples of past projects that have received excellent grades

74. What are the primary benefits of the appendix Ms. Baird will provide?
    a. More involvement of parents in school work; parent works with child, the teacher will have to spend less time re-teaching or explaining concepts again
    b. All components of the project will be included in the final submission; less time spent searching out missing work
    c. Students know how they will be graded and what is expected; students can take responsibility for their work.
    d. Students can see what constitutes an excellent project.

75. The 2nd-graders are required to learn their math facts for addition, subtraction and multiplication. They take timed tests each week to measure how many facts they can remember within five minutes. Many students have become discouraged and frustrated with their scores on the tests, since initially they are very low. What modifications might the teacher make?
    a. Do away with timed tests as a measure for math facts and switch to another form of assessment.
    b. Measure each student's improvement in retention each week so that they can see how much they have improved, rather than giving a flat percentage.
    c. Do not make modifications; students learn best with this type of assessment and grading and must be patient with the process.
    d. Do not show students their percentages or graded tests; rather discuss the process with them individually and let them know whether they have improved or not.

Use the scenario below to answer questions 76 and 77.
    Dareon occasionally displays a negative attitude about assignments. When his teacher introduces activities, he will say things like "this is going to be so boring" or "it's too hard." Dareon is an intelligent student, but often lacks the willingness or ability to see assignments through to completion. He will even have trouble starting his work because he will become upset about the assignment(s). Every now and then, other students will pick up on Dareon's attitude and begin to complain themselves.

76. What should Dareon's teacher do first to engage him in solving the problem?
    a. Immediately challenge Dareon's statements by saying things such as "No way—it is going to be fun!" or "Dareon, you are smart enough to do anything you want to do."
    b. Tell Dareon that his comments are unacceptable and unproductive. He can express himself, but should do so in his journal or outside of class, where he classmates will not be affected.
    c. Speak to Dareon's parents about his negative attitude and help them understand how it is affecting his performance in class. Enlist their help in dealing with his approach to learning since they know him best.
    d. Work to encourage and provide praise for each part of Dareon's efforts. Help break the work down into smaller segments so he can manage them. Point out his smaller successes and his efforts with praise and encouragement.

77. Once Dareon's attitude and class performance have begun to improve, how should the teacher follow up with Dareon to ensure continued success?

   a. Require Dareon to put one penny in a jar each time he makes a negative statement about his work. Once the jar is full, call an after-class meeting with him and possibly his parents to discuss the problem.

   b. Check in weekly with Dareon's parents to let them know how he is doing in class and whether or not his attitude has improved.

   c. Talk with Dareon regarding his feelings about his work and help him connect the steps taken to the positive results. Encourage him to speak positively about his abilities to help increase his confidence.

   d. Simply ignore negative behaviors and reward positive behaviors with free time or treats. Dareon will learn through conditioning that positive behaviors are more desirable and lead to academic success.

78. Which strategy would be least effective in engaging parent involvement in the classroom?

   a. Sending a letter describing volunteer needs, descriptions, parameters, and times specified for volunteer opportunities

   b. Linking certain kinds of parental involvement to specific benefits during parent orientation

   c. Making phone calls or spending time talking with parents informally to build parent-teacher relationships

   d. Holding parent-education workshops so that parents can understand what their children are learning in class and how they can become involved

79. For those parents who want to volunteer in Mrs. Davis' 3rd-grade classroom, what activity would be the most beneficial?

   a. Assign a parent to assist students who are having difficulty in class and may need extra attention.

   b. Allow parents to lead an activity, lesson, or discussion based on areas of personal expertise.

   c. Delegate responsibilities such as updating the class website, lamination, organizational tasks, and other non-teaching activities to volunteer parents.

   d. Enlist parents to participate in surveys and discussions about their children's learning experiences to get feedback on how to improve classroom instruction.

80. Mr. Aemon teaches elementary-aged students. He holds parent conferences twice a year and tries to talk with parents in person as often as he can. How can he supplement this type of communication so that parents are more aware of what their children are doing in class on a daily basis?

   a. Use email to communicate individual daily and weekly progress.

   b. Incorporate a weekly goal sheet that includes pre-planned lessons and individual student progress on assignments and tests; goal sheets are checked and signed by both the teacher and parents each week.

   c. Increase the number of parent conferences held each year.

   d. Ask students to journal about their class work, grades, and progress; send journals home once per week so parents can read about the child's experience in class.

81. Which choice describes a/the purpose for assessment in the classroom?

   a. To diagnose student learning needs

   b. To evaluate effectiveness of instruction and curriculum

   c. To monitor all students' progress

   d. All of the above

82. Which statement is false?
a. Assessment should be ongoing and provide information that spans a period of time, rather than isolated or discreet points in time.
b. Educators should use educational values and objectives as the foundations for assessment design.
c. The most effective assessments are observational and personal in nature; descriptions should be recorded by an educator who knows the student well.
d. Assessments should be used to monitor patterns in student and teacher performance.

83. A teacher uses a variety of un-graded assignments and quizzes to help guide her instructional decisions through units of instruction. This type of assessment would be described as:
a. Formative
b. Summative
c. Narrative
d. Diagnostic

84. Ms. Nesbit requires her middle-school Social Studies students to keep their class notes in a binder. She regularly checks the notes to assess how well students are processing main ideas and central themes. How can she use these binders further to assess students' critical thinking, writing and analytical skills?
a. Require all students to add a section to their binders in which they will place records of class discussions.
b. At the end of each class period, ask students to record their thoughts and opinions on what they have learned in a journal-style entry in their binders.
c. Allow students to write their own versions of historical events as though they had occurred in modern times at the end of each week.
d. Assign written work that requires application and analytical skills; students keep class work in their binders to be checked along with their notes.

Use the information below to answer questions 85 and 86.

> In class this month, students will be studying a variety of particularly complex human anatomy processes. It is important for each student to grasp the placement and functions of various anatomical organs and systems first. These concepts are the foundation for study of more complex processes in later lessons.

85. Which choice provides the best aid for instruction in the classroom?
a. Assign one body part and function to each student, to be presented to the class one at a time.
b. Provide a sturdy, clear, color-coded anatomy chart to each student, upon which he or she can place labels and take notes.
c. Distribute pre-typed lecture notes to students so that they can focus on listening to what the teacher is saying rather than on capturing the notes.
d. Show a video on the material from reading assignments to help solidify knowledge.

86. How should the teacher use the correct teaching aid from Question 85 for purposes of assessment?
a. Use a rubric to grade each student's presentation and gauge understanding of the topic.
b. Check over student progress on anatomy charts as lectures progress to ensure that students have foundations for future lessons.
c. Monitor student focus, body language, and verbal responses during lecture and discussions.
d. Ask students to write down major concepts from the video and assigned readings.

87. All students are required to take a graduation exam. Student performance on this exam is measured against a pre-determined set of learning objectives. Those students who pass the test are permitted to graduate. The graduation exam is a:
    a. norm-referenced test.
    b. non-standardized test.
    c. student performance assessment.
    d. criterion-referenced test.

88. Which of the following is not a benefit of creating and using student portfolios?
    a. Individual student performance and progress can be compared to other students in a systematic, informative way.
    b. Teachers, administrators, and parents gain comprehensive understanding of student abilities and progress.
    c. Students learn to think critically about what they have learned in the past.
    d. Test-taking skills and/or anxiety are eliminated as obstacles in evaluating student abilities.

Consider the information below to answer questions 89 and 90.
    I.   Short-answer response
    II.   Essay response
    III.   Multiple-choice question
    IV.   True/False question
    V.   Matching tables

89. Which combination of items would be most effective for evaluating student mastery of factual knowledge and ability to apply the knowledge?
    a. III and V
    b. I and II
    c. II and III
    d. IV and V

90. Which item could be based on discussion, evaluation, or comparison?
    a. IV
    b. V
    c. III
    d. II

91. A test's _____ is typically determined by temporal stability, form equivalence and internal consistency.
    a. Validity
    b. Efficacy
    c. Reliability
    d. Grade median

92. Which of the following is an example of an invalid test?

a. A teacher administers a pop quiz containing fact-recall questions based on the previous week's lessons.

b. Teenagers have to pass a written test and demonstrate driving skills to a state employee in order to get a driver's license.

c. Students are permitted to work together to determine what concepts were most valuable and should be included on the next unit test.

d. A standardized test measures students' mastery of concepts in math, language, and science each year.

93. As Ms. Williams is recording student grades on the last unit test, she notices that a high number of students made an 85%; in fact, 85% is the highest grade in the class. When she looks at the tests again, she realizes that most students received incorrect marks on the same three questions. Which statement is most likely to be true?

a. The students probably cheated on the test, causing them to miss the same questions.

b. The high-frequency mode alerted Ms. Williams to possible problems with test questions.

c. Ms. Williams will have to identify the cause(s) for the abnormal median values in order to prove the test's reliability.

d. Standard error of measurement suggests that Ms. Williams should use a grading curve to improve student grades.

94. At the end of each school year, all students at Hank's school take a standardized test. Hank's parents have just received his most recent scores. Hank scored in the 75th percentile in language and in the 98th percentile in math. Hank:

a. scored as well or better than 75% of students who took the test in language; he scored as well or better than 98% of students who took the test in math.

b. answered 75% of language questions correctly and 98% of math questions correctly.

c. ranked 75th in language and 98th in math compared to other students who took the test.

d. scored one standard deviation higher in math than he did in language.

95. The local paper runs a story about the most recent round of standardized tests given in the public school system. The reporter points out that there are large gaps between scores of ESL (English as a second language) students and non-ESL students. This report is based on…

a. an un-reliable test.

b. unethical and unauthorized access to students' confidential records

c. disaggregated test data

d. inaccurate generalization of test data

Use the information below to answer questions 96 through 98.

Emily is starting 2nd grade this year. Her teacher, Ms. Martin, has looked over her records from last year and notes that Emily's standardized test scores are somewhat lower than average. Ms. Martin learns from Emily's previous teacher that she has a very hard time sitting still and finishing her work. Emily often daydreams or seems "tuned out" during lesson time. Her previous teacher spoke to Emily's parents to discuss the problem; they agreed that part of the problem may simply be Emily's young age, and that they should continue to work with her at home and encourage her as much as possible to focus on her school work.

96. How can Ms. Martin ensure that she starts the year off in a positive and beneficial manner for Emily's sake?

    a. Call Emily's parents to discuss the need for psycho-educational before school starts. Emphasize the importance of starting the year off strong and not wasting any more time.

    b. If possible, do a home visit to begin building a relationship with Emily and her family, as well as to find out as much as possible about Emily's likes, dislikes, habits, and history.

    c. Knowing that Emily likely suffers from ADD or ADHD, plan lesson and classroom modifications for her such as assigned seating, shorter assignments and lessons, and untimed testing.

    d. Recommend Emily for special services through the school district based on test scores and the previous teacher's observations.

97. Before speaking with Emily's parents (at any point during the year) about a need for further educational testing, Ms. Martin should:

    a. ensure that she has at least one witness to the conversation in the event that Emily's parents become angry.

    b. educate herself on the testing and intervention process so that she can be a resource and support for the family.

    c. create a detailed list of Emily's symptoms and problems, as well as a log of incidents in the classroom, to show Emily's parents how vital this intervention process is.

    d. talk to Emily about her problems with focus and attention. Learn how she feels about the issues and share this information with her parents.

98. When speaking with Emily's parents, Ms. Martin should emphasize that the purpose of psycho-educational testing is:

    a. to determine which class and teacher would be the best fit for Emily.

    b. to ensure that Emily is on the right type and dosage of medication to fit her needs.

    c. to identify the causes of Emily's educational obstacles and find the best interventions to fit her needs.

    d. to provide proof to the school district and insurance companies that Emily should be provided with special services and/or medication.

99. Which statement is most likely to be true?

    a. All teachers should do whatever is necessary to acquire basic knowledge of common symptoms of special needs in children, as well as typical interventions and strategies for instructing high-needs students.

    b. Teachers are always the most equipped individuals to determine a child's individual needs and interventions; however, most schools require evaluation by a professional.

    c. All children should be considered "high-needs;" teachers should teach each child as though he or she may have learning difficulties when instructing and guiding them.

    d. Students with learning or physiological challenges are best served in separate classrooms, where they can get the specialized attention and services they deserve.

100. Which of the following professionals is least likely to work directly with high-needs students in the classroom?

    a. Pediatrician
    b. Occupational therapist
    c. Speech-language pathologist
    d. Counselor

Answer Key and Explanations

1. C: It is usually beneficial for teachers to share information about what concepts students will learn in class. Depending on the age and abilities of the students, it may even be helpful to provide a timeline of concepts and assignments in the form of a syllabus. By sharing this information with students, they can understand the purpose behind what they are learning, thus increasing personal responsibility in the learning process. Students can also use these shared learning goals to evaluate their own understanding whenever needed. Once all topics are covered, the teacher may also choose to use the conceptual framework and timeline as a tool for review.

2. B: Homework can function as an important extension of classroom instruction. Ideally, students will learn the process of taking responsibility for their own learning and will recognize the importance of continuing the learning process outside the classroom. Teachers are present to instruct and guide during class, but students can and should review concepts outside class to transfer them to long-term memory. Students also have the opportunity to apply both old and new knowledge to new situations outside class, or during homework. The best type of homework includes both review and opportunities for transfer of knowledge.

3. A: Maintaining a framework for class objectives is very important before planning or evaluating effectiveness of lessons. The teacher must determine first what concepts need to be addressed during the course. He will then need to create corresponding measures of assessment for these objectives. In other words, he will decide ahead of time how to measure whether or not his objectives are being achieved. Once the objectives and assessment techniques have been created, the teacher can refer to them when he wants to analyze whether or not the method of instruction is functioning effectively.

4. C: Students demonstrate mastery over a period of time. True mastery is the ability to understand and apply knowledge in various circumstances over the course of time (rather than on just one occasion). By changing circumstances and increasing length of time for demonstration of mastery, teachers can ensure that the student has retained knowledge in long-term memory and understands it well enough to use it in a variety of contexts. Therefore, the teacher will need to look at a variety of contexts when determining student mastery. Some students do well on tests but have trouble during class discussions, or vice versa. Often, a student will retain knowledge for a short period of time and not be able to recall it. By using a varied approach to student assessment, the teacher will gain a better understanding of what each student has mastered.

5. B: All subjects are connected in various forms. The two teachers are coordinating instruction in a way that will foster activation of prior knowledge. Students will learn about historical events and how those events affected social norms and ideas at the time. Written texts will provide opportunities for students to apply what they have learned in history and identify how historical events are reflected in literary art. They will be able to make connections between factual/historical knowledge and real examples from texts. The language and history teachers' combined efforts will also leave more time and space for students to reflect and discuss deeper meaning in what they are learning.

6. B: Students sometimes face challenges in understanding the difference between a generalization and a specific concept. But it is important that students learn to analyze ideas for specificity and be able to identify those that are generalized. This example requires students to think analytically about the form and function of each object, and discuss these objects with peers. The students will help each other learn to understand how different people may think about an object and that their analyses may not agree. As they sort themselves, students will learn how to agree upon general ideas or objects through experience. Explaining their methods to the class will solidify the thinking process for each student group.

7. A: This type of instruction employs several valuable techniques. Limiting the number of words introduced in each unit will reduce the temptation to memorize or skim over the lesson contents. The students will be more likely to retain the meaning, spelling and usage of each word if they practice them repeatedly over time. By introducing the words in a variety of subject contexts, the students will also gain a more thorough understanding of how each word functions in language. The teacher can use various lessons to show the students patterns in the way certain words are spelled or used, also deepening the students' understanding of the words.

8. D: Many teachers are given extensive curriculum mandates by school administration. Each teacher is then charged with bringing that material to life in a way that excites and engages students. As the teacher presents the curriculum strands, she has to find a way to get the students to participate. Each aspect of the curriculum can serve as foundation for an activity to get the students involved, such as a skit or debate. The more participatory the class is (as opposed to lecture-style instruction), the more likely it is that students will engage in critical thinking about what they have learned. Students are also more likely to have fun with the material than they would with purely teacher-centered instruction.

9. C: The question prompt emphasizes that curriculum objectives must be both clear and measurable. In order to fit this criterion, the objective has to be easily understood and there must be an obvious way to evaluate whether or not the objective has been met. In this choice, students are expected to learn the steps of the Scientific Method in conceptual form. The instructor can measure whether or not this concept has been mastered by evaluating each student's independent project. This is the only choice that provides both the intended learning outcome and its form of measurement.

10. A: In the question prompt, the teacher gets the students involved by soliciting their input about the subject of Art. He then aligns their contributions with the concepts he hopes they will master during the term. By inviting certain projects to be posted on the felt boards, the teacher is giving the students visual examples of what each concept might mean for an individual experiencing art. The felt boards also provide opportunities for discussion and collaboration among students, in a systematic way. Each concept is specifically outlined and remains constant throughout the course; only the examples change.

11. C: Each board contains one major concept, or content cluster. The ideas posted are general and will allow students to review their primary course objectives at any point. By changing the works posted on each board, the teacher provides a visual opportunity for students to evaluate art pieces and their own responses to them. Students can also evaluate how strongly they agree or disagree with the relationship between the pieces and the ideas, thus deepening their understanding of the course objectives.

12. D: *Chunking* is a teaching technique that relates similar concepts to one another. Through chunking, individuals learn to associate facts, objects or ideas that have common traits; they also learn to categorize their new knowledge intellectually. In this lesson, the teacher shows students how to "chunk" information in their note-taking. Each main idea or concept goes to the left of the line and supporting or related information is placed on the right. This demonstration models the process of associating related pieces of information. Chunking will theoretically help students understand and recall information more readily over the course of time.

13. A: At any given time, an individual can focus, or "attend to," a limited number of tasks or concepts. The information currently being attended to is stored in short-term memory, which has limited capacity. However, once information is transferred to long-term memory, it can likely be retained and retrieved for an unlimited period of time. Good teachers will find ways to help students move information from short- to long-term memory, using memorization, applications, self-monitoring, retrieval tools, and more. By increasing information stored in long-term memory, individuals can build on prior learning and associate new concepts into pre-existing mental categories (or chunks).

14. A: Repetition is an important technique for increasing mastery of skills, especially when students are learning a great deal of information at one time. However, it is impossible to repeat and re-teach all information taught during a term. Repetition should be used thoughtfully and on the right concepts. It will be useful for a teacher to re-introduce concepts that students may have mastered at one time, but that they do not utilize in class often. The longer students go without utilizing information, the harder it will be to retrieve when they need to do so. Teachers will likely not need to review detailed examples or preview material consistently, as these do not serve her overall curriculum goals. It will also be impossible to review every detail or example each day; rather, a review of major concepts would be more helpful.

15. B: Graphic organizers and visual displays are vital to reaching all types of learners. Each student learns differently and some concepts are easier to understand when using two-dimensional organizers. Venn diagrams consist of two overlapping ovals or circles, creating three separate spaces for students to record ideas. The outer areas can be used to identify differences in objects or ideas; the overlapping area is intended for their similarities.

16. B: Many students have trouble identifying cause and effect relationships inside text, especially when the relationships are not overtly stated. Students who are learning English may have an especially difficult time with this skill. Often, teaching students about linking words will help them pick out relevant information in longer, more challenging texts. Once they know which words should draw their attention, they will be more equipped to identify the components of the concept and relationship.

17. D: Howard Gardner first introduced the concept of multiple intelligences. His theory rests on the idea that there are multiple ways to understand or 'to know.' Every individual will have strengths and weaknesses in learning, but everyone will learn in different ways. The seven commonly identified intelligences are: verbal/linguistic, existential, logical/mathematical, interpersonal, intrapersonal, visual/spatial, musical/rhythmic, bodily/kinesthetic, and naturalist. Each intelligence can be used to help identify the way in which a student understands the world around him or her.

18. C: Students comprehend reading material more easily when given the appropriate previewing tools. In order for discussion of student beliefs about a subject (choice C) to be relevant, there must be additional communication about what they are expected to learn and how to increase reading comprehension. Choices A, B and D provide clear and applicable tools for increasing comprehension through previewing. These tools also help students organize the information for better comprehension and retention.

19. B: Student attitudes about subject material will affect how much they can and will learn. In this case, Ms. Hanks is using past experience to predict possible barriers to student learning. By incorporating a variety of activities into her lessons, she will lessen the monotony of a less-entertaining subject and engage the students' interest. She will also increase the likelihood of information retention by making the lessons fun and informative at the same time. The more actively the students participate, the more likely it is that they will have better attitudes and gain a better understanding of the material.

20. A: The KWL technique includes three components. Students are asked to identify what they already know about a given subject. The next step involves deciding what each person wants to learn in the presentation, lesson or assigned reading. Finally, students will determine what they have learned and analyze how this information relates to what was recorded in previous steps.

21. C: The KWL technique can be used to achieve several outcomes. The two primary purposes for using KWL are improving comprehension of material and increasing self-monitoring of comprehension in the individual. Students learn how to take control of the comprehension process during guided or independent work and identify how effectively they understand what they are learning. Self-monitoring will assist students in determining further areas for study or other learning needs.

22. A: Detailed curriculum can be challenging to teach effectively, given multiple barriers to student learning: focus and engagement can diminish with long periods of complex instruction. The lesson plan described includes a variety of contexts in which students can internalize the concepts. The teacher includes review of concepts to help increase retention each day, as well as a short presentation of the day's concepts. Giving the students a break will allow them to take care of personal needs and refocus their energy in class. Group practice will allow students to understand the concepts through doing, rather than listening, and will encourage peer feedback and assistance. Finally, the class discussion will correct any mistakes and serve as an interim review for the day.

23. D: All students will relate personal experience to course objectives in different ways. In fact, some students may not instinctively apply personal knowledge to what they are learning unless encouraged to do so frequently. By keeping a personal journal, students can thoroughly explore what they have learned in class, as well as ideas or experiences that can be connected to that content. Students will be more likely to feel comfortable expressing personal concepts if the forum is private (a journal that will only be seen by the teacher and student) and if the format is flexible (being able to draw or write).

24. A: All classroom activities have direct and indirect purposes. At times, a teacher may choose not to share objectives with students in order to increase independent thinking. The teacher should identify the purpose for a new learning activity so that students understand what they are doing and why. By talking about the activity fully during the day or two before starting, students will have ample notice of upcoming events, but not so much discussion that their anxiety levels will increase as a result. Giving notice will allow students to prepare for the quizzes but will not allow enough time to over-prepare.

25. B: When teaching a new group of students, the teacher must design instruction that will be at an appropriate level of challenge. If course work is too easy or too challenging, the students may lose confidence and interest early on. If samples of past work or performance on tests are available, the teacher should review these whenever possible. Doing so will give him or her insight into the students' past instruction and abilities. However, the teacher should also be sure to provide a current assessment of some type to account for changes in classroom environment and knowledge retention. The teacher should ensure that students meet objectives for the end of the term or course, but will need to begin at an ability-appropriate level for the students.

26. C: Teachers must not only plan instructional content, but the sequence of instruction as well. This sequencing can be founded in various formats, as long as the presentation is logical and can be explained easily to another person. However, if students show that they understand a concept fully, there is no need to present it as such during class. It is important to resist the urge to teach curriculum simply because it has been outlined and planned ahead of time. Presenting previously mastered material would waste valuable teaching time and would fail to further student progress.

27. B: Some concepts will take longer than one or two lesson periods to teach, but can be covered in a relatively short period of time. However, some skills are complex enough that several weeks should be dedicated to learning them. Writing a research paper involves several steps, including defining a topic, forming a question, gathering research, evaluating and organizing findings, composing a draft, proofing and editing the draft and learning elements of style and composition. Each component of the task involves multiple skills that may be new for some students. This type of project should be broken down into smaller, more manageable components so that teachers can organize information effectively and students will grasp each important skill.

28. C: Problem-solving skills are complex and often not intuitive for many learners. However, there are countless creative ways to teach these skills. The best variety of instruction will include presentation of problem-solving frameworks and strategies as well as activities in which students can utilize those skills. Some students may also benefit from seeing ineffective ways of solving problems and tools to correct mistakes. Often, personal problems that students face can be inappropriate for class discussion. Some students may also feel uncomfortable sharing problems with the class. Ultimately, including this time in lesson plans will not guarantee that students are learning directly from the problems presented, as they would in other activities.

29. C: Group problem-solving can be very effective in building skills. However, students should be assessed individually to account for any gaps in understanding, especially since they will be evaluated individually on standardized tests. Problem-solving skills are based on a process rather than simply finding a correct answer; for this reason, assessments should take into account not only solutions but methods used to find solutions. In combination with standardized test scores, these weekly assignments will provide a complete picture of how well students are internalizing the skills taught in class.

30. D: Vocabulary instruction is vital to mastery of all subject areas. Regardless of context, vocabulary should be part of dynamic instruction rather than rote memory or definition. The final choice includes several important components. First, the teacher engages the students in defining the words for themselves, utilizing prior knowledge activation as well as reference skills. Incorporating the game will encourage student participation and interest. Finally, students will be more likely to retain information with the multi-sensory game: they will see, hear, and physically create meanings for the words.

31. D: During the concrete phase, students will learn concepts using objects that they can see, feel and manipulate. For example, a student might first learn to add, subtract, or multiply by manipulating beads or jacks. Representational lessons use representations (not symbols or abstractions) of the physical objects used during the concrete phase. For example, students might use pictures of the beads and jacks to answer math questions on paper, thus bridging the transition between concrete and abstract phases.

32. A: The CRA approach is meant to help students learn in a variety of contexts, as well as in a systematic way. There are many signs that a child is ready to move toward the abstract: demonstrating mastery of earlier phases, asking to practice abstractly or making independent connections between concepts. However, part of the concrete phase is learning and practicing with concrete materials. While the student in choice A was able to re-demonstrate what he or she had been shown, the student may have needed additional practice with concrete objects before moving to representational or abstract phases.

33. A: Teachers should regularly work to identify patterns of understanding of course material (or lack thereof). However, formal testing is usually not frequent enough to serve as the only form of assessment. Waiting until test time minimizes a teacher's chances to re-present or clarify concepts. Introducing in-class "comprehension checks" will allow the teacher to evaluate student understanding without taking time away from instruction; additionally, the teacher will also be able to modify instruction immediately to increase understanding. Participation or engagement does not always signify understanding, especially if the topic presented is interesting for students.

34. B: Scaffolding is a technique intended to provide diverse methods of instruction for students and gradual withdrawal of teacher assistance. In the initial phases of scaffolding, the teacher guides students on class concepts or activities. He or she helps motivate and instruct the students, often modeling problem-solving, ideas and steps. Over time, the teacher reduces involvement in dealing with the concepts so that students can become more independent in the learning process.

35. C: Using extensions is a vital part of classroom instruction: students must have opportunities to take the learning process beyond information presented by the teacher inside the classroom. All students need opportunities to use what they have learned in class and apply (or extend) the information to other skill areas. The third choice provides students with a direct application of classroom material on *biodiversity* by observing plants and animals at the lake. Students also incorporate journaling and research techniques to complement their studies. Finally, each entry must incorporate classroom material so that students are making connections between what they have learned and their current activities.

36. C: Metaphors and analogies are often taught in Language courses, but can be useful teaching tools in all subjects. When a teacher presents new concepts, he or she can use these tools to help students compare them to previously-learned information. For example, the teacher might help students understand how their eyes work by comparing them to a camera. Metaphors and analogies use slightly different language to accomplish the same goal: comparing two unlike things. However, one method need not be used before or in place of another.

37. B: Abstract concepts must be taught in a variety of ways to facilitate student mastery. It can be difficult to know whether or not students completely understand the concepts, given size and complexity. By asking students to explain ideas in their own words, the teacher will gain insight about how well the students internalized the material. The teacher will also be able to tell if the most important information has been mastered, since the students will be giving answers that directly reflect their perceptions of the content.

38. A: Once a teacher has determined what learning outcomes are intended, he or she must design instruction to facilitate those specific outcomes. There are times when certain types of instruction will be more effective than others; also, introducing variety in instructional design will help maintain student interest and engagement. It is likely that students will need some guidance and help when they do anything for the first time, especially something as complex as a science experiment. By placing students into small groups, the teacher will facilitate cooperative learning and peer guidance, thus allowing her more time and freedom to help students who need it.

39. B: Group-based activities are beneficial for inspiring creative thinking, cooperative learning and student engagement. However, students must learn how to work effectively in groups over time. The teacher in this scenario requires students to determine specific roles within the group. This requirement will cut down on confusion in the early stages of the activity as students try to agree on who will be responsible for what tasks. Students may also experience less frustration since every individual will have responsibility (preventing some students from getting credit for minimal participation). Not only will the group work be more accurate and efficient, but students will achieve the indirect aim of the assignment, which is to strengthen their abilities to cooperate with one another.

40. D: Effective questioning techniques are always important in the classroom. Simply asking questions often is not sufficient for maximizing the usefulness of classroom questions. There are many points at which a teacher might use carefully selected questions to accomplish a number of goals. Questions can be used to gauge student comprehension of a particular topic or lesson content (choice A). Pausing lecture to ask questions can also re-focus the instruction and engage students who may have become distracted (choice B). By asking the right questions in the right format, a teacher can encourage students to think critically about a subject and apply what they have previously learned (choice C).

41. C: The student in this scenario could be asking a question for a variety of reasons. He or she may not have been paying attention, resulting in a gap in understanding later in class. The student may even have been paying attention during class, but simply missed the specific piece of information being discussed (since students cannot possibly hear and remember every part of a class lecture or activity). The student may not have understood the information based on how it was communicated. Allowing another student to answer the question not only validates the information as important, but helps the teacher know whether or not others in the class understood what was presented. The teacher also refrains from shaming the student for not hearing or understanding a concept, which is common for all students at one point or another.

42. A: The most effective questions are specific in nature, even if the desired response should be elaborative or complex. Asking more than one question at once can have counter-productive effects on the learner. The student may be overwhelmed by hearing multiple questions at once and could feel anxious about being able to answer all of them. This type of questioning may also make it difficult for the student to sequence or communicate ideas verbally. If a student is uncomfortable answering a question, it will be more effective to give him or her time to answer, and then move on to a new question or choose another student to answer.

43. C: In this scenario, students will have more time to think critically about the material during homework than they would during class time (since questions can be on-the-spot in nature). By requiring the students to write their questions down, the teacher will have better insight about the level of comprehension each student possesses. Providing peer-created questions to the class will prompt students to think critically about the subject and will present examples of age-appropriate ways to think about the material. This activity should be led by the teacher, rather than students, since she needs to be assured of student comprehension.

44. D: Certain types of questions facilitate critical thinking. Elaborating questions encourage students to think beyond a concrete, specific answer. By asking students to elaborate on a topic or previous answer, the student will need to think about what they already know and expand upon it either verbally or in writing. Convergent and closed questions invite more specific, factual answers that can often be found in text or notes. Clarifying questions might require critical thinking; however, this type of question may simply require the student to make certain answers more specific in nature.

45. D: Student engagement and comprehension begins to ebb after a short period of time. Although it is impossible to say exactly how long each student can stay actively engaged, most studies agree that the average attention span is shorter than the average class period. Direct, teacher-guided instruction is usually necessary in order to present concepts. However, this style of instruction will lead to disengagement if not paired with other types of activities. By alternating teacher-directed and student-directed activities, students will be less likely to become bored or distracted. Including group and individual formats will also provide variety and increase the number of contexts within which students can transfer their knowledge.

46. C: Young children at a Kindergarten or 1st-grade level are still learning to sit still, read and write fluently, and increase attention spans. For these reasons, the classroom environment should provide a variety of activities and seating spaces. Certain activities require certain body positions; for instance, when writing, students should be seated at a desk of the appropriate height, but for a group lesson or discussion, students might be able to sit in a circle on the floor. In this choice, each activity determines the type of seating and space allotted, increasing likelihood that students will achieve the intended learning outcomes.

47. B: No singular classroom arrangement is likely to be appropriate for the whole of a class term. The best classroom instruction is based on purposeful instruction and variety to keep students engaged. In choice B, the classroom is set up to facilitate the type of activity going on that week. Changing the type of instruction and the physical space will prevent classes from becoming boring and predictable. Students are more likely to stay focused and interested if they are learning in different ways over time. This approach also allows the teacher to cater to various learning styles (visual, kinesthetic, auditory).

48. A: Writing poetry is a challenging task and should be considered a very personal art form. It is impossible for students to learn about all kinds of poetry, poets, methods, functions of the art form in just a month. However, choice A achieves a number of learning outcomes. Each student will learn about one individual who has been successful in creating poetry. The assignment will also show students the connections between a person's life experiences and the writing they create. The teacher gives each student the option to either present a poem by the poet creatively or write an original work in the style of that poet. This choice allows students to interpret and present poetry in a personal way, but gives them the opportunity to play to individual strengths (i.e. writing, reading, performing).

49. B: *Rehearsal* refers to the practice of repeating information or making concepts more memorable by repetition. In choice B. students are using a combination of music and repetition to remember concepts that might otherwise be difficult to retain. Songs will make detailed concepts memorable by incorporating not only memory but auditory and physical processes as well. Most students will learn songs more easily, as compared to only simple memorization, and are more likely to retain the information over a long period of time.

50. D: Many students experience performance anxiety in school that is related to assessments, public speaking, or tendency toward perfectionism. Teachers have the unique opportunity to work with students and help them strive toward excellence while diminishing fear of failure. All of the choices in this scenario might be helpful for students. Creating a variety of assignments will play to different strengths in each student, allowing all students the chance to succeed and build skill in weaker areas. Relationships with students will help the teacher find ways to motivate students through tougher or less interesting work by relating material to personal interests. Finally, teachers can always talk with individual students about perceived failures and help them learn from current circumstances, as well as accept that no one will ever achieve 'perfection' during the learning process.

51. A: Classroom rules are important and necessary. Whenever a group of individuals must share a space and resources while working toward a common goal, there will be conflicts or difficult circumstances. Rules are helpful in creating norms amongst any social group and will help ease anxiety in uncomfortable situations. However, members of any group are most likely to abide by the rules if they can participate in creating them; when students have a say in what rules are appropriate, they will probably take more ownership over time. Students will feel as though their feelings and needs have been addressed, or in the least 'heard,' and assist in enforcing rules in class.

52. C: The question prompt provides several clues about what may have happened in this situation. If Holly's work had just been incorrect, it may have been an indication that she simply did not understand the concepts. However, the prompt states that her work was incorrect and also very sloppy and that this is unusual for Holly. Therefore, it is probably best for Mr. Croft to speak with her and encourage her to do her best, rather than penalize her. If the sloppy work were turned in frequently, perhaps a lecture and low grade would be appropriate. But all students will have times in which they do not do their best. The teacher can use those moments to show students that it is always better to make an effort than not. Offering a maximum of 80% on the assignment will show Holly that her actions do have consequences, although she can achieve a much better score by making an effort.

53. A: Students should learn that their classroom is a community and that they can all play a role in making it better. Each student should have opportunities to do both desirable and less desirable tasks in order to build confidence and a sense of responsibility within a group. Rotating jobs allows students to identify what types of duties are most appealing to them. All students will have occasions where their work habits and behavior are positive, just as there will be times when they are negative. Responsibility should not be assigned based on school performance, since students must learn to take responsibility at all times for themselves and their communities.

54. C: Morning routines are important for students at every level. The way the day begins sets the tone for the remainder of class lessons and activities. The teacher in this scenario is obviously prepared, since the agenda and materials have already been established and made accessible. The teacher is therefore able to greet each student personally at the beginning of the day. By doing this, the teacher is building relationships with students, gauging the moods and attitudes of the students, and establishing her leading presence in the classroom. There will likely be less confusion and chaos since the teacher is there to direct the start to the day.

55. D: Some conflict is inevitable when students are discussing topics in class. In fact, the presence of disagreements indicates that students are thinking critically about a subject and are interested enough to participate in discussion, both of which are ideal in a classroom setting. Teachers must be careful not to 'shut down' conflicts simply because they can be uncomfortable. These situations provide opportunities to teach problem-solving and conflict-resolution. During this type of conversation, students will also refine their thinking about a subject and learn to express themselves more clearly when speaking. If students become overly personal in their speech, or begin to accuse or attack one another, the teacher should immediately intervene and offer to mediate the conversation outside of class. The follow-up conversation is important so that the students involved feel 'heard' and can find resolution for their issues, which could potentially affect class performance if not handled correctly.

56. B: Positive reinforcement and encouragement are vital for students in the learning process. Some students are more easily motivated or discouraged than others. However, many common responses by parents and teachers can devalue the student's intrinsic self-confidence by placing the locus of the reward outside the student. For instance, telling a student "I'm proud of you" teaches him or her to look to an outside individual for reward on a job well done. While the sentiment may be true, and very positive, intrinsic confidence and motivation are built by helping the student feel pride in his or her own accomplishments. The second choice points out an accomplishment, but focuses on the student's own feelings of pride and completion, rather than those of an outside source.

57. A: Several aspects of this prompt are important in understanding the best approach. It is common for students at this age to have trouble staying seated and focused for long periods of time. Therefore, all approaches should be based on the assumption that the child is not necessarily abnormal until the behavior becomes patterned and debilitative *despite* creative classroom strategies. The student is not only neglecting his own work but keeping others from focusing as well. Alternating physical activity and school work will give the boy breaks to release physical energy and help "ground" himself for the work at hand. He may also feel more able to complete the work if it is broken down into smaller, more manageable segments.

58. D: As a high-school student, Mira should be capable of discussing the classroom issues with her teacher. She is also old enough to start learning that she must be responsible for her behavior and school work, albeit with the help of an instructor or guide. There might be many reasons for Mira's disengagement, none of which her teacher will know without speaking to her and getting to know her. She may be disinterested in the subject matter, distracted by home life, not feeling well, or struggling in school. Whatever the problem, the teacher will be more equipped to handle the situation when she understands its causes more thoroughly.

59. B: Misconduct in class can be frustrating for teachers who must accomplish challenging goals each day. Student misbehavior can impede instruction and harmony in the classroom. However, students are still children; they are still learning to understand how their actions affect others. Children are also incapable of exhibiting consistent or perfect self-control. Teachers must incorporate instruction into their plans that helps students build better behavior skills. Direct, varied instruction, combined with clear and consistent consequences, will help students learn how to behave in desired ways inside the classroom.

60. A: Many undesired behaviors are common in class, regardless of a student's age. Students will inevitably get off-task during class time. It is impossible to stay focused each day for long periods of time without 'mental breaks' or distraction. The teacher can assist Harry and Nina non-verbally because they are not intentionally hurting other students and are likely not thinking about the consequences of their actions (failing to finish their work). By clearing her throat, catching their attention to give them a pointed 'look,' or simply moving nearer to them, the teacher will probably be able to remind the students of their task without creating unnecessary discord.

61. D: In this scenario, all students in the class are being affected by excessive talking and classroom conflicts. Students are missing out on vital instruction and becoming distracted by personal problems in class. This group of students is old enough to participate in solving these problems and should be held accountable for doing so. Class meetings highlight the importance of working cooperatively to solve problems and create a forum for sharing potential solutions. Also, having students help create expectations and consequences will increase their personal responsibility for meeting goals. As the guiding adult, Mrs. Norris should refrain for over-directing the process and should focus on building self-confidence and teaching students how to resolve their conflicts.

62. C: This scenario provides an excellent ongoing opportunity to build problem-solving skills and character among students. Since the initial plans were laid out during a cooperative class meeting, the entire class should be involved in monitoring improvements. In this way, students can evaluate the effectiveness of their plans. Journal writing can be an effective tool in this situation, as it provides a safe space for students to explore personal feelings. However, group discussion is most likely to help students continue their collaborative efforts and improvements.

63. D: Students should always be warned that *time-out* is a potential consequence of their actions. The purpose behind this approach should always be to give the student time to think about his or her actions and to understand that certain behaviors are unacceptable in class. This consequence should never be used to shame or torture the child; therefore, it should always be connected to the undesired behavior before and after the event. By warning and then debriefing the child, he or she will have a better understanding of why the removal from the group was necessary. Forcing the child to apologize or to sit in repeated *time-outs* defeats the purpose of engaging the child in understanding and striving for better behavior.

64. A: Review for the test is often its own reward; students are able to refresh memory on important topics and may have an easier time studying for the test. However, the first approach creates a fun environment in which to review. Students also have opportunities to collaborate with one another and help make connections between prior and current knowledge. The academic bowl reinforces the notion that the practice and review is important for its own sake and that the reward is intrinsic. However, providing a treat for the winning team provides an additional incentive and makes the game a bit more fun.

65. A: Class discussion does not always flow easily. Student participation can be affected by mood, energy level, understanding of the material, and confidence in answering questions in front of the class. Instead of forcing students to answer, or suggesting that they have failed to pay attention, the teacher should try to understand how capable they are of discussing the material. It may be that his first question was a bit too complex for initial discussion. The teacher should start off with simple, direct questions that students can answer easily and that will provide background for more complex discussions. He can then build up to other topics that require logic and interpretation.

66. D: Homework can be a controversial subject amongst educators. Students spend countless hours at school and extracurricular activities and some adults disagree on the usefulness of homework as an educational tool. Designed correctly, homework can help reinforce work done in class, as well as teach students to take responsibility for mastering material. The homework assigned in choice D contains a variety of assignments that will keep students engaged. By giving the homework a monthly time frame, students can also choose how and when they complete the assignments; this choice helps them take control of the process and use it in the most helpful way. Good homework assignments are not "busy-work," but rather include work that will accomplish a variety of purposes (practice, application, preview, and so on).

67. D: If teachers want students to complete homework assignments on their own time, it follows that teachers should make use of the returned work to help further the learning process. However, grading large quantities of homework can interfere with other grading and planning time. This choice allows for flexibility for students and teachers alike. The teacher in this case provides examples of how students should journal about their homework—this method requires students to complete work and to think critically about what they are learning from it. Teachers can also check journals for indications of growth and mastery over time.

68. B: Rewards and recognition can be useful tools in education, but should not be the sole focus of each activity. Growth and learning should be the primary goals of any assignment. However, most students respond positively to recognition of their work. If teachers focus on positive, controllable aspects of student work, those students will be more likely to understand that effort, attitude, consistency, and other traits are beneficial in the learning process. This model also allows teachers to recognize all students, rather than limiting rewards to students who achieve correct or positive results on the first attempt. The recognition in choice B focuses on actions that will help the students in the long-term and can be applied without discrimination.

69. C: The teacher wants to use an incentive, or positive motivator, to help children complete their class work. Some students will have a hard time curbing their desires to talk and have fun with friends in order to get their work done, especially if they do not find the work interesting or challenging. However, some students may be more motivated to complete work if they know they will have social or outdoor time later on. This motivator is ideal because it is directly related to what the students want and should be fairly easy to attain. Incentives should be attainable, clear, and related to the task at hand; providing extra time for homework is not likely to motivate students who are not yet even completing class work. Whenever possible, teachers should avoid providing token rewards that are unhealthy or whose appeal will wear off after time, such as candy.

70. D: All students must learn over time that there are consequences for their actions. However, it is important not to shame or unduly criticize students for their behavior, since they are still growing and learning what behaviors are acceptable. Linda and Ellie's teacher chose a consequence that was directly related to their inappropriate action: since they worked together, they each got half the grade. The consequence for cheating was to fail the exam, but the teacher made a point about their behavior with the way she chose to handle the situation. The teacher also prevented the same scenario from happening again by assigning different seats for the girls for future individual work.

71. C: Tyler's participation is important and should not be discouraged. He has obviously learned that participation is beneficial, but has not yet learned to prepare and to use his critical thinking skills effectively during discussion. In this situation, talking to Tyler about the problem might embarrass him or discourage him from contributing in class. Talking to the entire class about providing evidence and explanations for answers will model the appropriate processes, which can help all students improve skills. All students will learn how to back up answers with textual information and logic, including Tyler. Ideally, he will learn along with classmates to prepare answers carefully and thoughtfully.

72. B: All students have different capabilities and capacities for learning. But teachers should not be in the habit of raising and lowering expectations for individuals based on these factors; doing so would unnecessarily limit or put pressure on individual students. There may be times when teachers must *change* individual expectations for students or assignments, but disadvantage or disability does not mean that students can never achieve intended learning outcomes. Each class activity must have intended learning goals and/or purposes in order to have meaning and create growth. In rare occasions, most of the group will try to complete an activity and fail to do so. The teacher should use these instances to examine his or her own expectations for reasonability and efficacy, and change or lower them accordingly. However, teacher expectations for student *capacity* should not change; he or she should maintain high expectations for all students.

73. C: Students will be working on this project for a long period of time—several months. They are also learning to manage time, learn about a subject and present information in a variety of contexts. The grading rubric will include all components of the project so students can manage their time. The rubric also describes what constitutes poor, fair, good, or excellent work within each component.

74. C: Providing a rubric will generate several benefits. All components will be included on the rubric so that students can keep track of each part of the assignment. Students will also be able to understand what constitutes good work in each area by reading descriptions of expectations at each level. The rubric will allow students to manage themselves to teacher expectations while also learning to take control of the completion process.

75. B: Timed tests can be intimidating for many students, and demoralizing for still others. The teacher does not necessarily need to change her form of assessment. Timed tests are an effective way of measuring how many facts a student can remember quickly; quick recall of facts is important when working on more complex math operations. However, the teacher can show the students that she expects them to improve over time, rather than to be perfect while still learning. By measuring improvement over time, rather than giving flat percentages on the tests, the teacher models encouragement and the desire for progress over time for her students. Ideally, students will relax as they see gains in learning throughout the class.

76. D: Students usually make comments about work being boring or difficult when they lack confidence. Even bright students will sometimes need encouragement to follow through on their work, especially if they are concerned that it will be too difficult. Dareon needs help in recognizing that his attitude is not helpful in getting his work done, as well as in figuring out how to get started on his assignments. Breaking the work down into smaller pieces and praising his efforts (rather than the overall outcome, which may be overwhelming for him at first) will help make his tasks a bit less daunting. Over time, his success will likely build his confidence and ability to motivate himself.

77. C: Dareon's teacher should make sure to help him identify which actions were helpful in achieving his goals. By praising efforts over outcome, he will begin to see the effects of a positive attitude and hard work. The teacher can also encourage him to speak positively to himself; positive self-talk will have a significant effect on a student's confidence if done consistently. The teacher must function as a model for encouragement and engaging students in motivating themselves, rather than for punishment and negativity.

78. A: Many parents want to be involved in their child's education, or at the very least are open to the notion that becoming involved will benefit their child. However, most parents do not have the educational expertise or flexibility of schedule that allows them to be at school during the day. Setting up strict parameters about involvement is more likely to discourage parents from being involved. However, building personal relationships, explaining the benefits of involvement, and being flexible about scheduling is more likely to encourage involvement. The more parents know about what is happening in class, the more likely they will be to identify ways in which they can help.

79. B: Parents usually have areas of individual expertise or knowledge, often related to their chosen professions. Parent-led workshops or lessons provide variety of instruction and incorporate specialized activities that the teacher may lack the knowledge or time to create for her class. Students have the benefit of learning from a variety of individuals with different teaching styles. Parents also benefit from getting to know the students in class and getting an idea of how the children are progressing in skills such as critical thinking.

80. B: Most teachers and parents recognize that communication is vital to ensuring student success. However, most adults, especially teachers, lack the time needed to communicate with individual families on a frequent basis. A goal sheet is the most realistic way to give parents daily and weekly updates on progress without creating an unrealistic schedule for communication. The teacher can pre-record lessons and activities that have been planned for the students. Each student can then keep track of what he or she has done in class, grades, and other markers to be checked by both the teacher and the parents each week. Parents receive more information without burdening the teacher with copious amounts of extra work.

81. D: Assessment is a vital component of both teaching and learning. All curriculum design must begin with establishment of goals and objectives. Assessment allows educators to determine how well these goals have been met. The purpose of assessing student progress serves a variety of functions in addition to providing grades. Teachers can identify any gaps in student learning; make decisions about future instruction; assess original goals; and more. Assessments can also be used to evaluate teachers' performance and identify professional development goals.

82. C: There are countless forms of assessment: formal and informal, graded and un-graded, observational and standardized. Educators should utilize a variety of formats to evaluate student needs and progress, rather than focusing on one method. While observational assessment can be very beneficial in some cases, all students should be given a variety of assignments/tests to measure and describe their learning experiences. Each type of assessment provides different kinds of insight into the complex processes that take place in education.

83. A: Formative assessment is typically used during the process of instruction. Formative evaluations allow teachers to gauge student progress for purposes of monitoring and modifying instruction. These assignments are usually not graded, although at times there may be exceptions to this rule. Summative assessment is used at the end of a grading term or instructional unit to provide a summary of how well a student grasped and retained concepts.

84. B: The question prompt identifies the teacher's desire to evaluate not only students' factual retention through note-taking, but their critical-thinking and writing skills, as well. Adding a reflection-based journal entry provides the teacher with a way to gauge student progress in all areas without adding extra notebooks or complicated assignments. Thus, as she reads over student notes, she will be able to tell whether or not students understood important concepts, but also how they reflect on these concepts. The journal entries will also provide a record of students' skills over time in all areas.

85. B: The initial information describes lesson content as complex and detailed; students must understand a large quantity of information in a relatively short period of time in order to progress in class. Concepts can be classified in many ways, and in this case, should be considered "spatial." Human anatomy is spatial in nature, meaning that students can process information based on how concepts relate to one another in space. Since students will be learning first about parts of the body and their functions, it makes sense to provide students with a spatial aid to help them understand where the parts are located. The spatial representation of the body will also help students understand how systems and organs are related to one another. Re-creating images of the body would be time-consuming, so the teacher has provided the charts such that students can focus on labeling and annotating rather than drawing.

86. B: The anatomy charts are visual and spatial; therefore, they provide a quick method of assessing how well students have understood material. The teacher can easily look over students' charts throughout lecture and group work to ensure that no one has missed vital information or incorrectly annotated the charts. If need be, charts can be turned in and then checked after class. Since the information presented is vital to the next phase of instruction, the teacher has a vested interest in making sure that students have the best tools possible.

87. D: Students are often required to take a variety of exams as the progress through school; most students will have some form of standardized testing during this time. Criterion-referenced tests are based on a pre-determined set of concepts or objectives. Test questions are organized around these concepts and student performance should indicate individual levels of mastery. By contrast, norm-referenced tests measure student performance by comparing student scores to other student scores; the measure of competency is based on comparison to other students, rather than to pre-determined objectives.

88. A: Student portfolios can be helpful in the process of teaching and of learning. Portfolios typically include samples of student work in a variety assignment formats. These samples will also represent student progress over a period of time, rather than of one sitting or type of assignment. Portfolios provide a broad range of work from which to understand a student's capabilities. Students should also be involved in selecting work for portfolios; by doing so, each student can construct meaning from his or her own learning experiences, identifying work that is personally meaningful. However, portfolios are not typically useful in comparing students, since the selection of work is individual in nature. Students may use different types of work and cannot be compared systematically to one another using this type of tool.

89. C: Test items can and should vary based on the type of information being tested. Each type of item response should closely match the teacher's objectives in administering assessment. In this case, the teacher wants to understand how well students have mastered a quantity of factual material *and* how well each student can apply the knowledge. In order to test these skills in a realistic amount of time, the teacher should use more than one type of test question. Multiple-choice questions are most effective in gauging knowledge about specific concepts, and can be used for testing factual knowledge. Essay questions provide freedom for students to demonstrate synthesis or critical-application skills. In this type of question, students can show the teacher how well they are able to use what they have learned to solve problems or apply knowledge.

90. D: Essay questions can be categorized in a variety of ways. Good essay questions should provide test-takers with a specific task, such as discussing an idea, evaluating a concept for validity, comparing two ideas, or expressing opinions about a subject. Questions can be categorized as such so that students have guidelines with which to answer the question; essay questions that are too broad may cause students to leave out important information when they write. Ultimately, the goal of essay-writing is to demonstrate synthesis and application skills. Essay test items should be linked to specific objectives (such as discussion, comparison, or evaluation) in order to be effective for test-takers or evaluators.

91. C: Not all tests are created equal; some tests may not be effective in measuring student performance due to issues such as unreliability or validity. Test reliability refers to the level of consistency in test scores over time, or with respect to other variables in testing subjects or environment. Reliability is determined by how consistent test scores are over time (temporal consistency) and across different test formats (form equivalence), as well as how consistent test-item responses are within the same test (internal consistency).

92. C: Validity of a test refers to its ability to measure what it is intended to measure. A valid test is one that addresses the intended learning objectives in a consistent way. Students may have ideas about what information they value or find useful; in fact, this exercise would be an effective tool for understanding student progress and perception in class. However, a unit test is usually designed to measure mastery of specific objectives over time. If students create the test content, the test cannot be said to accurately measure objectives, since students themselves did not create or analyze course objectives in this case.

93. B: The most-repeated number in a set of data is called the mode. In this case, Ms. Williams notes that the mode, 85%, is showing up frequently in her grades. The question prompt also suggests that most of the students answered the same questions incorrectly and that none of the students exceeded the 85%. It is likely that there was a problem with those specific questions, such as vague wording or failure to address material in class, causing most students to miss them. Therefore, the mode score alerted Ms. Williams to a pattern in student responses; from this point she can work to determine the cause and a plan of action. While it is possible that students cheated on their tests, this cannot be proven by scores alone and choice B would still be correct.

94. A: A percentile rank is often confused with other kinds of test measurement. Percentile is the number below which a certain percentage of data points are placed after all data values are divided into 100 components. In essence, all test scores in one data set are divided into 100 components in order to get percentile rankings. For example, Hank's ranking of the 75th percentile means his test scores fall at or above 75% of the other test scores in that data set. Hank scored as well or better than75% of students in language and 98% of students in math.

95. C: Aggregated data provides general, summative information on a group of values or scores. In this scenario, aggregated scores would consist of all students' scores combined. Disaggregated test score data is based on scores within subsets, such as gender, socio-economic status or nationality. This reporter wrote about a specific group of scores and their relationship to the whole. The story points out differences in the scores of ESL students when compared to students who speak English as a first language. The reporter used disaggregated data to make his point.

96. B: All Ms. Martin knows before starting school is that Emily struggles with focus and follow-through on her work. She also knows that Emily's test scores are lower than average. However, she cannot know yet why Emily was struggling. Ms. Martin does not yet have a relationship with the student or with her parents, which should preclude her from making assumptions about causes of the problem or possible interventions. The causes of the focus problem may be related to age, diet, family life, chemical imbalance, sensory problems, or a variety of other factors. Ms. Martin should attempt to get to know Emily and her family as quickly and thoroughly as possible to begin making plans for how to work with Emily. By knowing more about the student, the teacher may be able to find strategies that will help Emily focus and make progress; building these relationships will also create a trust between teacher and family that will be beneficial in the event that Emily needs further testing or help outside the classroom.

97. B: Ms. Martin may find that the strategies and interventions she has tried are not working for Emily. In some cases, students truly need further evaluation from an outside professional to determine physiological or educational problems. If Ms. Martin wants to recommend this path, she should make sure that she is educated on how the process works. It is likely that Emily's parents will have questions about the implications of further testing, as well as cost, time frames, and the way this information will be used at school. The more Ms. Martin knows about the process, the more she can support and guide the family through what can be a stressful time. Ms. Martin will also be able to implement strategies recommended by the testing facility and partner with the doctors and parents more effectively if she has educated herself beforehand.

98. C: Many teachers and families misperceive the function of psycho-educational testing. Some adults fear that their children will be labeled or inappropriately placed within the school or school system. Teachers and parents have likely seen cases in which a student has been inaccurately diagnosed, leading to a variety of issues during schooling. However, students with learning difficulties can benefit greatly from accurate diagnosis. The purpose of finding the right diagnosis is not merely to 'label' a child, but to identify appropriate interventions to help the child thrive. Often, appropriate interventions will allow children to remain in their normal classrooms and learn with the simplest of modifications.

99. A: The field of education is constantly changing; the same is true of policies and regulations pertaining to children with special needs. Teachers are usually the first people to identify or intervene when a child is struggling in class. Every teacher should be responsible for educating him- or herself regarding possible problems that children might face. Without knowledge of symptoms, it will be impossible for a teacher to guide the student or parents effectively. The teacher may also find that previous knowledge of typical classroom strategies may benefit the child in question more quickly, and may prevent problems from getting worse.

100. A: Countless kinds of professionals are available to work with students in the classroom, including: occupational therapists, speech and language pathologists, counselors, paraprofessionals, and specialized therapists for specific disorders. Procedures for classroom interventions will vary by school and system; however, most classrooms now hold some children who are differently-abled or who have special needs. This change means that outside professionals will often work with students in class. However, pediatricians are not typically found in classrooms. These doctors are usually involved in the educational process for specific patients, but are not the experts most qualified to work with students on a day to day basis in the classroom.

Secret Key #1 – Time is Your Greatest Enemy

To succeed on the Principles of Learning and Teaching you must use your time wisely. Many students do not finish at least one section. This assessment is designed to test the beginning teacher's knowledge of job-related information.

There are four tests that cover the same fundamental topics and concepts, but, every test differs from the others by presenting developmentally appropriate cases. Every test contains four case histories. Each case history presents a teaching situation followed by 3 short-answer questions dealing with an area of teaching within the case history. There are short answer questions. A specific theory or book does not need to be cited but answers will be graded according to professionally acceptable principles and techniques. Be sure to answer all portions of the question. Each short answer question is allotted 25 minutes. The questions are scored 0-2.

Twenty four multiple choice questions are also included. They are not associated with the case histories. Ten minutes are allowed for each 12 question section.

The format of the test was discussed above, the contents are as follows:

Students as Learners   35% of total score
- Students as diverse learners
- Student learning environment and motivation
- Student development and the learning process

Instruction and Assessment   35% of total score
- Strategical planning
- Strategical instruction
- Strategical assessment

Communication Techniques   15% of total score
- Cultural and gender differences
- Effective verbal and nonverbal communication
- Stimulating discussion and responses in the classroom

Teacher Professionalism   15% of total score
- The reflective practitioner
- The larger community

As you can see, the time constraints are brutal. To succeed, you must ration your time properly.

Pace Yourself

Wear a watch. At the beginning of the test, check the time (or start a chronometer on your watch to count the minutes), and check the time after every few questions to make sure you are "on schedule."

If you are forced to speed up, do it efficiently. Usually one or more answer choices can be eliminated without too much difficulty. Above all, don't panic. Don't speed up and just begin guessing at random choices. By pacing yourself, and continually monitoring your progress against your watch, you will always know exactly how far ahead or behind you are with your available time. If you find that you are one minute behind on the test, don't skip one question without spending any time on it, just to catch back up. Take 15 fewer seconds on the next four questions, and after four questions you'll have caught back up. Once you catch back up, you can continue working each problem at your normal pace.

Furthermore, don't dwell on the problems that you were rushed on. If a problem was taking up too much time and you made a hurried guess, it must be difficult. The difficult questions are the ones you are most likely to miss anyway, so it isn't a big loss. It is better to end with more time than you need than to run out of time.

Lastly, sometimes it is beneficial to slow down if you are constantly getting ahead of time. You are always more likely to catch a careless mistake by working more slowly than quickly, and among very high-scoring test takers (those who are likely to have lots of time left over), careless errors affect the score more than mastery of material.

Secret Key #2 - Guessing is not Guesswork

You probably know that guessing is a good idea - unlike other standardized tests, there is no penalty for getting a wrong answer. Even if you have no idea about a question, you still have a 20-25% chance of getting it right.

Most test takers do not understand the impact that proper guessing can have on their score. Unless you score extremely high, guessing will significantly contribute to your final score.

Monkeys Take the Test

What most test takers don't realize is that to insure that 20-25% chance, you have to guess randomly. If you put 20 monkeys in a room to take this test, assuming they answered once per question and behaved themselves, on average they would get 20-25% of the questions correct. Put 20 test takers in the room, and the average will be much lower among guessed questions. Why?
1. The test writers intentionally writes deceptive answer choices that "look" right. A test taker has no idea about a question, so picks the "best looking" answer, which is often wrong. The monkey has no idea what looks good and what doesn't, so will consistently be lucky about 20-25% of the time.
2. Test takers will eliminate answer choices from the guessing pool based on a hunch or intuition. Simple but correct answers often get excluded, leaving a 0% chance of being correct. The monkey has no clue, and often gets lucky with the best choice.

This is why the process of elimination endorsed by most test courses is flawed and detrimental to your performance- test takers don't guess, they make an ignorant stab in the dark that is usually worse than random.

$5 Challenge

Let me introduce one of the most valuable ideas of this course- the $5 challenge:

You only mark your "best guess" if you are willing to bet $5 on it.
You only eliminate choices from guessing if you are willing to bet $5 on it.

Why $5? Five dollars is an amount of money that is small yet not insignificant, and can really add up fast (20 questions could cost you $100). Likewise, each answer choice on one question of the test will have a small impact on your overall score, but it can really add up to a lot of points in the end.

The process of elimination IS valuable. The following shows your chance of guessing it right:

If you eliminate wrong answer choices until only this many remain:	1	2	3
Chance of getting it correct:	100%	50%	33%

However, if you accidentally eliminate the right answer or go on a hunch for an incorrect answer, your chances drop dramatically: to 0%. By guessing among all the answer choices, you are GUARANTEED to have a shot at the right answer.

That's why the $5 test is so valuable- if you give up the advantage and safety of a pure guess, it had better be worth the risk.

What we still haven't covered is how to be sure that whatever guess you make is truly random. Here's the easiest way:
Always pick the first answer choice among those remaining.

Such a technique means that you have decided, **before you see a single test question**, exactly how you are going to guess- and since the order of choices tells you nothing about which one is correct, this guessing technique is perfectly random.

This section is not meant to scare you away from making educated guesses or eliminating choices- you just need to define when a choice is worth eliminating. The $5 test, along with a pre-defined random guessing strategy, is the best way to make sure you reap all of the benefits of guessing.

Secret Key #3 - Practice Smarter, Not Harder

Many test takers delay the test preparation process because they dread the awful amounts of practice time they think necessary to succeed on the test. We have refined an effective method that will take you only a fraction of the time.
There are a number of "obstacles" in your way to succeed. Among these are answering questions, finishing in time, and mastering test-taking strategies. All must be executed on the day of the test at peak performance, or your score will suffer. The test is a mental marathon that has a large impact on your future.

Just like a marathon runner, it is important to work your way up to the full challenge. So first you just worry about questions, and then time, and finally strategy:

Success Strategy

1. Find a good source for practice tests.
2. If you are willing to make a larger time investment, consider using more than one study guide- often the different approaches of multiple authors will help you "get" difficult concepts.
3. Take a practice test with no time constraints, with all study helps "open book." Take your time with questions and focus on applying strategies.
4. Take a practice test with time constraints, with all guides "open book."
5. Take a final practice test with no open material and time limits

If you have time to take more practice tests, just repeat step 5. By gradually exposing yourself to the full rigors of the test environment, you will condition your mind to the stress of test day and maximize your success.

Secret Key #4 - Prepare, Don't Procrastinate

Let me state an obvious fact: if you take the test three times, you will get three different scores. This is due to the way you feel on test day, the level of preparedness you have, and, despite the test writers' claims to the contrary, some tests WILL be easier for you than others.
Since your future depends so much on your score, you should maximize your chances of success. In order to maximize the likelihood of success, you've got to prepare in advance. This means taking practice tests and spending time learning the information and test taking strategies you will need to succeed.

Never take the test as a "practice" test, expecting that you can just take it again if you need to. Feel free to take sample tests on your own, but when you go to take the official test, be prepared, be focused, and do your best the first time!

Secret Key #5 - Test Yourself

Everyone knows that time is money. There is no need to spend too much of your time or too little of your time preparing for the test. You should only spend as much of your precious time preparing as is necessary for you to get the score you need.
Once you have taken a practice test under real conditions of time constraints, then you will know if you are ready for the test or not.

If you have scored extremely high the first time that you take the practice test, then there is not much point in spending countless hours studying. You are already there.

Benchmark your abilities by retaking practice tests and seeing how much you have improved. Once you score high enough to guarantee success, then you are ready.

If you have scored well below where you need, then knuckle down and begin studying in earnest. Check your improvement regularly through the use of practice tests under real conditions. Above all, don't worry, panic, or give up. The key is perseverance!

Then, when you go to take the test, remain confident and remember how well you did on the practice tests. If you can score high enough on a practice test, then you can do the same on the real thing.

General Strategies

The most important thing you can do is to ignore your fears and jump into the test immediately- do not be overwhelmed by any strange-sounding terms. You have to jump into the test like jumping into a pool- all at once is the easiest way.

Make Predictions

As you read and understand the question, try to guess what the answer will be. Remember that several of the answer choices are wrong, and once you begin reading them, your mind will immediately become cluttered with answer choices designed to throw you off. Your mind is typically the most focused immediately after you have read the question and digested its contents. If you can, try to predict what the correct answer will be. You may be surprised at what you can predict.

Quickly scan the choices and see if your prediction is in the listed answer choices. If it is, then you can be quite confident that you have the right answer. It still won't hurt to check the other answer choices, but most of the time, you've got it!

Answer the Question

It may seem obvious to only pick answer choices that answer the question, but the test writers can create some excellent answer choices that are wrong. Don't pick an answer just because it sounds right, or you believe it to be true. It MUST answer the question. Once you've made your selection, always go back and check it against the question and make sure that you didn't misread the question, and the answer choice does answer the question posed.

Benchmark

After you read the first answer choice, decide if you think it sounds correct or not. If it doesn't, move on to the next answer choice. If it does, mentally mark that answer choice. This doesn't mean that you've definitely selected it as your answer choice; it just means that it's the best you've seen thus far. Go ahead and read the next choice. If the next choice is worse than the one you've already selected, keep going to the next answer choice. If the next choice is better than the choice you've already selected, mentally mark the new answer choice as your best guess.

The first answer choice that you select becomes your standard. Every other answer choice must be benchmarked against that standard. That choice is correct until proven otherwise by another answer choice beating it out. Once you've decided that no other answer choice seems as good, do one final check to ensure that your answer choice answers the question posed.

Valid Information

Don't discount any of the information provided in the question. Every piece of information may be necessary to determine the correct answer. None of the information in the question is there to throw you off (while the answer choices will certainly have information to throw you off). If two seemingly unrelated topics are discussed, don't ignore either. You can be confident there is a relationship, or it wouldn't be included in the question, and you are probably going to have to determine what is that relationship to find the answer.

Avoid "Fact Traps"

Don't get distracted by a choice that is factually true. Your search is for the answer that answers the question. Stay focused and don't fall for an answer that is true but incorrect. Always go back to the question and make sure you're choosing an answer that actually answers the question and is not just a true statement. An answer can be factually correct, but it MUST answer the question asked. Additionally, two answers can both be seemingly correct, so be sure to read all of the answer choices, and make sure that you get the one that BEST answers the question.

Milk the Question

Some of the questions may throw you completely off. They might deal with a subject you have not been exposed to, or one that you haven't reviewed in years. While your lack of knowledge about the subject will be a hindrance, the question itself can give you many clues that will help you find the correct answer. Read the question carefully and look for clues. Watch particularly for adjectives and nouns describing difficult terms or words that you don't recognize. Regardless of if you completely understand a word or not, replacing it with a synonym either provided or one you more familiar with may help you to understand what the questions are asking. Rather than wracking your mind about specific detailed information concerning a difficult term or word, try to use mental substitutes that are easier to understand.

The Trap of Familiarity

Don't just choose a word because you recognize it. On difficult questions, you may not recognize a number of words in the answer choices. The test writers don't put "make-believe" words on the test; so don't think that just because you only recognize all the words in one answer choice means that answer choice must be correct. If you only recognize words in one answer choice, then focus on that one. Is it correct? Try your best to determine if it is correct. If it is, that is great, but if it doesn't, eliminate it. Each word and answer choice you eliminate increases your chances of getting the question correct, even if you then have to guess among the unfamiliar choices.

Eliminate Answers

Eliminate choices as soon as you realize they are wrong. But be careful! Make sure you consider all of the possible answer choices. Just because one appears right, doesn't mean that the next one won't be even better! The test writers will usually put more than one good answer choice for every question, so read all of them. Don't worry if you are stuck between two that seem right. By getting down to just two remaining possible choices, your odds are now 50/50. Rather than wasting too much time, play the odds. You are guessing, but guessing wisely, because you've been able to knock out some of the answer choices that you know are wrong. If you are eliminating choices and realize that the last answer choice you are left with is also obviously wrong, don't panic. Start over and consider each choice again. There may easily be something that you missed the first time and will realize on the second pass.

Tough Questions

If you are stumped on a problem or it appears too hard or too difficult, don't waste time. Move on! Remember though, if you can quickly check for obviously incorrect answer choices, your chances of guessing correctly are greatly improved. Before you completely give up, at least try to knock out a couple of possible answers. Eliminate what you can and then guess at the remaining answer choices before moving on.

Brainstorm

If you get stuck on a difficult question, spend a few seconds quickly brainstorming. Run through the complete list of possible answer choices. Look at each choice and ask yourself, "Could this answer the question satisfactorily?" Go through each answer choice and consider it independently of the other. By systematically going through all possibilities, you may find something that you would otherwise overlook. Remember that when you get stuck, it's important to try to keep moving.

Read Carefully

Understand the problem. Read the question and answer choices carefully. Don't miss the question because you misread the terms. You have plenty of time to read each question thoroughly and make sure you understand what is being asked. Yet a happy medium must be attained, so don't waste too much time. You must read carefully, but efficiently.

Face Value

When in doubt, use common sense. Always accept the situation in the problem at face value. Don't read too much into it. These problems will not require you to make huge leaps of logic. The test writers aren't trying to throw you off with a cheap trick. If you have to go beyond creativity and make a leap of logic in order to have an answer choice answer the question, then you should look at the other answer choices. Don't overcomplicate the problem by creating theoretical relationships or explanations that will warp time or space. These are normal problems rooted in reality. It's just that the applicable relationship or explanation may not be readily apparent and you have to figure things out. Use your common sense to interpret anything that isn't clear.

Prefixes

If you're having trouble with a word in the question or answer choices, try dissecting it. Take advantage of every clue that the word might include. Prefixes and suffixes can be a huge help. Usually they allow you to determine a basic meaning. Pre- means before, post- means after, pro - is positive, de- is negative. From these prefixes and suffixes, you can get an idea of the general meaning of the word and try to put it into context. Beware though of any traps. Just because con is the opposite of pro, doesn't necessarily mean congress is the opposite of progress!

Hedge Phrases

Watch out for critical "hedge" phrases, such as likely, may, can, will often, sometimes, often, almost, mostly, usually, generally, rarely, sometimes. Question writers insert these hedge phrases to cover every possibility. Often an answer choice will be wrong simply because it leaves no room for exception. Avoid answer choices that have definitive words like "exactly," and "always".

Switchback Words

Stay alert for "switchbacks". These are the words and phrases frequently used to alert you to shifts in thought. The most common switchback word is "but". Others include although, however, nevertheless, on the other hand, even though, while, in spite of, despite, regardless of.

New Information

Correct answer choices will rarely have completely new information included. Answer choices typically are straightforward reflections of the material asked about and will directly relate to the question. If a new piece of information is included in an answer choice that doesn't even seem to relate to the topic being asked about, then that answer choice is likely incorrect. All of the information needed to answer the question is usually provided for you, and so you should not have to make guesses that are unsupported or choose answer choices that require unknown information that cannot be reasoned on its own.

Time Management

On technical questions, don't get lost on the technical terms. Don't spend too much time on any one question. If you don't know what a term means, then since you don't have a dictionary, odds are you aren't going to get much further. You should immediately recognize terms as whether or not you know them. If you don't, work with the other clues that you have, the other answer choices and terms provided, but don't waste too much time trying to figure out a difficult term.

Contextual Clues

Look for contextual clues. An answer can be right but not correct. The contextual clues will help you find the answer that is most right and is correct. Understand the context in which a phrase or statement is made. This will help you make important distinctions.

Don't Panic

Panicking will not answer any questions for you. Therefore, it isn't helpful. When you first see the question, if your mind goes blank, take a deep breath. Force yourself to mechanically go through the steps of solving the problem and using the strategies you've learned.

Pace Yourself

Don't get clock fever. It's easy to be overwhelmed when you're looking at a page full of questions, your mind is full of random thoughts and feeling confused, and the clock is ticking down faster than you would like. Calm down and maintain the pace that you have set for yourself. As long as you are on track by monitoring your pace, you are guaranteed to have enough time for yourself. When you get to the last few minutes of the test, it may seem like you won't have enough time left, but if you only have as many questions as you should have left at that point, then you're right on track!

Answer Selection

The best way to pick an answer choice is to eliminate all of those that are wrong, until only one is left and confirm that is the correct answer. Sometimes though, an answer choice may immediately look right. Be careful! Take a second to make sure that the other choices are not equally obvious. Don't make a hasty mistake. There are only two times that you should stop before checking other answers. First is when you are positive that the answer choice you have selected is correct. Second is when time is almost out and you have to make a quick guess!

Check Your Work

Since you will probably not know every term listed and the answer to every question, it is important that you get credit for the ones that you do know. Don't miss any questions through careless mistakes. If at all possible, try to take a second to look back over your answer selection and make sure you've selected the correct answer choice and haven't made a costly careless mistake (such as marking an answer choice that you didn't mean to mark). This quick double check should more than pay for itself in caught mistakes for the time it costs.

Beware of Directly Quoted Answers

Sometimes an answer choice will repeat word for word a portion of the question or reference section. However, beware of such exact duplication – it may be a trap! More than likely, the correct choice will paraphrase or summarize a point, rather than being exactly the same wording.

Slang

Scientific sounding answers are better than slang ones. An answer choice that begins "To compare the outcomes..." is much more likely to be correct than one that begins "Because some people insisted..."

Extreme Statements

Avoid wild answers that throw out highly controversial ideas that are proclaimed as established fact. An answer choice that states the "process should be used in certain situations, if..." is much more likely to be correct than one that states the "process should be discontinued completely." The first is a calm rational statement and doesn't even make a definitive, uncompromising stance, using a hedge word "if" to provide wiggle room, whereas the second choice is a radical idea and far more extreme.

Answer Choice Families

When you have two or more answer choices that are direct opposites or parallels, one of them is usually the correct answer. For instance, if one answer choice states "x increases" and another answer choice states "x decreases" or "y increases," then those two or three answer choices are very similar in construction and fall into the same family of answer choices. A family of answer choices is when two or three answer choices are very similar in construction, and yet often have a directly opposite meaning. Usually the correct answer choice will be in that family of answer choices. The "odd man out" or answer choice that doesn't seem to fit the parallel construction of the other answer choices is more likely to be incorrect.

Special Report: What Your Test Score Will Tell You About Your IQ

Did you know that most standardized tests correlate very strongly with IQ? In fact, your general intelligence is a better predictor of your success than any other factor, and most tests intentionally measure this trait to some degree to ensure that those selected by the test are truly qualified for the test's purposes.

Before we can delve into the relation between your test score and IQ, I will first have to explain what exactly is IQ. Here's the formula:

Your IQ = 100 + (Number of standard deviations below or above the average)*15

Now, let's define standard deviations by using an example. If we have 5 people with 5 different heights, then first we calculate the average. Let's say the average was 65 inches. The standard deviation is the "average distance" away from the average of each of the members. It is a direct measure of variability - if the 5 people included Jackie Chan and Shaquille O'Neal, obviously there's a lot more variability in that group than a group of 5 sisters who are all within 6 inches in height of each other. The standard deviation uses a number to characterize the average range of difference within a group.

A convenient feature of most groups is that they have a "normal" distribution- makes sense that most things would be normal, right? Without getting into a bunch of statistical mumbo-jumbo, you just need to know that if you know the average of the group and the standard deviation, you can successfully predict someone's percentile rank in the group.

Confused? Let me give you an example. If instead of 5 people's heights, we had 100 people, we could figure out their rank in height JUST by knowing the average, standard deviation, and their height. We wouldn't need to know each person's height and manually rank them, we could just predict their rank based on three numbers.

What this means is that you can take your PERCENTILE rank that is often given with your test and relate this to your RELATIVE IQ of people taking the test - that is, your IQ relative to the people taking the test. Obviously, there's no way to know your actual IQ because the people taking a standardized test are usually not very good samples of the general population- many of those with extremely low IQ's never achieve a level of success or competency necessary to complete a typical standardized test. In fact, professional psychologists who measure IQ actually have to use non-written tests that can fairly measure the IQ of those not able to complete a traditional test.

The bottom line is to not take your test score too seriously, but it is fun to compute your "relative IQ" among the people who took the test with you. I've done the calculations below. Just look up your percentile rank in the left and then you'll see your "relative IQ" for your test in the right hand column-

Percentile Rank	Your Relative IQ		Percentile Rank	Your Relative IQ
99	135		59	103
98	131		58	103
97	128		57	103
96	126		56	102
95	125		55	102
94	123		54	102
93	122		53	101
92	121		52	101
91	120		51	100
90	119		50	100
89	118		49	100
88	118		48	99
87	117		47	99
86	116		46	98
85	116		45	98
84	115		44	98
83	114		43	97
82	114		42	97
81	113		41	97
80	113		40	96
79	112		39	96
78	112		38	95
77	111		37	95
76	111		36	95
75	110		35	94
74	110		34	94
73	109		33	93
72	109		32	93
71	108		31	93
70	108		30	92
69	107		29	92
68	107		28	91
67	107		27	91
66	106		26	90
65	106		25	90
64	105		24	89
63	105		23	89
62	105		22	88
61	104		21	88
60	104		20	87

Special Report: What is Test Anxiety and How to Overcome It?

The very nature of tests caters to some level of anxiety, nervousness or tension, just as we feel for any important event that occurs in our lives. A little bit of anxiety or nervousness can be a good thing. It helps us with motivation, and makes achievement just that much sweeter. However, too much anxiety can be a problem; especially if it hinders our ability to function and perform.

"Test anxiety," is the term that refers to the emotional reactions that some test-takers experience when faced with a test or exam. Having a fear of testing and exams is based upon a rational fear, since the test-taker's performance can shape the course of an academic career. Nevertheless, experiencing excessive fear of examinations will only interfere with the test-takers ability to perform, and his/her chances to be successful.

There are a large variety of causes that can contribute to the development and sensation of test anxiety. These include, but are not limited to lack of performance and worrying about issues surrounding the test.

Lack of Preparation

Lack of preparation can be identified by the following behaviors or situations:

Not scheduling enough time to study, and therefore cramming the night before the test or exam
Managing time poorly, to create the sensation that there is not enough time to do everything
Failing to organize the text information in advance, so that the study material consists of the entire text and not simply the pertinent information
Poor overall studying habits

Worrying, on the other hand, can be related to both the test taker, or many other factors around him/her that will be affected by the results of the test. These include worrying about:

Previous performances on similar exams, or exams in general
How friends and other students are achieving
The negative consequences that will result from a poor grade or failure

There are three primary elements to test anxiety. Physical components, which involve the same typical bodily reactions as those to acute anxiety (to be discussed below). Emotional factors have to do with fear or panic. Mental or cognitive issues concerning attention spans and memory abilities.

Physical Signals

There are many different symptoms of test anxiety, and these are not limited to mental and emotional strain. Frequently there are a range of physical signals that will let a test taker know that he/she is suffering from test anxiety. These bodily changes can include the following:

Perspiring
Sweaty palms
Wet, trembling hands
Nausea
Dry mouth
A knot in the stomach
Headache
Faintness
Muscle tension
Aching shoulders, back and neck
Rapid heart beat
Feeling too hot/cold

To recognize the sensation of test anxiety, a test-taker should monitor him/herself for the following sensations:

The physical distress symptoms as listed above
Emotional sensitivity, expressing emotional feelings such as the need to cry or laugh too much, or a sensation of anger or helplessness
A decreased ability to think, causing the test-taker to blank out or have racing thoughts that are hard to organize or control.

Though most students will feel some level of anxiety when faced with a test or exam, the majority can cope with that anxiety and maintain it at a manageable level. However, those who cannot are faced with a very real and very serious condition, which can and should be controlled for the immeasurable benefit of this sufferer.

Naturally, these sensations lead to negative results for the testing experience. The most common effects of test anxiety have to do with nervousness and mental blocking.

Nervousness

Nervousness can appear in several different levels:

The test-taker's difficulty, or even inability to read and understand the questions on the test
The difficulty or inability to organize thoughts to a coherent form
The difficulty or inability to recall key words and concepts relating to the testing questions (especially essays)
The receipt of poor grades on a test, though the test material was well known by the test taker

Conversely, a person may also experience mental blocking, which involves:

Blanking out on test questions
Only remembering the correct answers to the questions when the test has already finished.

Fortunately for test anxiety sufferers, beating these feelings, to a large degree, has to do with proper preparation. When a test taker has a feeling of preparedness, then anxiety will be dramatically lessened.

The first step to resolving anxiety issues is to distinguish which of the two types of anxiety are being suffered. If the anxiety is a direct result of a lack of preparation, this should be considered a normal reaction, and the anxiety level (as opposed to the test results) shouldn't be anything to worry about. However, if, when adequately prepared, the test-taker still panics, blanks out, or seems to overreact, this is not a fully rational reaction. While this can be considered normal too, there are many ways to combat and overcome these effects. Remember that anxiety cannot be entirely eliminated, however, there are ways to minimize it, to make the anxiety easier to manage. Preparation is one of the best ways to minimize test anxiety. Therefore the following techniques are wise in order to best fight off any anxiety that may want to build.

To begin with, try to avoid cramming before a test, whenever it is possible. By trying to memorize an entire term's worth of information in one day, you'll be shocking your system, and not giving yourself a very good chance to absorb the information. This is an easy path to anxiety, so for those who suffer from test anxiety, cramming should not even be considered an option.

Instead of cramming, work throughout the semester to combine all of the material which is presented throughout the semester, and work on it gradually as the course goes by, making sure to master the main concepts first, leaving minor details for a week or so before the test.

To study for the upcoming exam, be sure to pose questions that may be on the examination, to gauge the ability to answer them by integrating the ideas from your texts, notes and lectures, as well as any supplementary readings.

If it is truly impossible to cover all of the information that was covered in that particular term, concentrate on the most important portions, that can be covered very well. Learn these concepts as best as possible, so that when the test comes, a goal can be made to use these concepts as presentations of your knowledge.

In addition to study habits, changes in attitude are critical to beating a struggle with test anxiety. In fact, an improvement of the perspective over the entire test-taking experience can actually help a test taker to enjoy studying and therefore improve the overall experience. Be certain not to overemphasize the significance of the grade - know that the result of the test is neither a reflection of self worth, nor is it a measure of intelligence; one grade will not predict a person's future success.

To improve an overall testing outlook, the following steps should be tried:

Keeping in mind that the most reasonable expectation for taking a test is to expect to try to demonstrate as much of what you know as you possibly can.
Reminding ourselves that a test is only one test; this is not the only one, and there will be others.
The thought of thinking of oneself in an irrational, all-or-nothing term should be avoided at all costs.
A reward should be designated for after the test, so there's something to look forward to. Whether it be going to a movie, going out to eat, or simply visiting friends, schedule it in advance, and do it no matter what result is expected on the exam.

Test-takers should also keep in mind that the basics are some of the most important things, even beyond anti-anxiety techniques and studying. Never neglect the basic social, emotional and biological needs, in order to try to absorb information. In order to best achieve, these three factors must be held as just as important as the studying itself.

Study Steps

Remember the following important steps for studying:

Maintain healthy nutrition and exercise habits. Continue both your recreational activities and social pass times. These both contribute to your physical and emotional well being.
Be certain to get a good amount of sleep, especially the night before the test, because when you're overtired you are not able to perform to the best of your best ability.
Keep the studying pace to a moderate level by taking breaks when they are needed, and varying the work whenever possible, to keep the mind fresh instead of getting bored.
When enough studying has been done that all the material that can be learned has been learned, and the test taker is prepared for the test, stop studying and do something relaxing such as listening to music, watching a movie, or taking a warm bubble bath.

There are also many other techniques to minimize the uneasiness or apprehension that is experienced along with test anxiety before, during, or even after the examination. In fact, there are a great deal of things that can be done to stop anxiety from interfering with lifestyle and performance. Again, remember that anxiety will not be eliminated entirely, and it shouldn't be. Otherwise that "up" feeling for exams would not exist, and most of us depend on that sensation to perform better than usual. However, this anxiety has to be at a level that is manageable.

Of course, as we have just discussed, being prepared for the exam is half the battle right away. Attending all classes, finding out what knowledge will be expected on the exam, and knowing the exam schedules are easy steps to lowering anxiety. Keeping up with work will remove the need to cram, and efficient study habits will eliminate wasted time. Studying should be done in an ideal location for concentration, so that it is simple to become interested in the material and give it complete attention. A method such as SQ3R (Survey, Question, Read, Recite, Review) is a wonderful key to follow to make sure that the study habits are as effective as possible, especially in the case of learning from a textbook. Flashcards are great techniques for memorization. Learning to take good notes will mean that notes will be full of useful information, so that less sifting will need to be done to seek out what is pertinent for studying. Reviewing notes after class and then again on occasion will keep the information fresh in the mind. From notes that have been taken summary sheets and outlines can be made for simpler reviewing.

A study group can also be a very motivational and helpful place to study, as there will be a sharing of ideas, all of the minds can work together, to make sure that everyone understands, and the studying will be made more interesting because it will be a social occasion. Basically, though, as long as the test-taker remains organized and self confident, with efficient study habits, less time will need to be spent studying, and higher grades will be achieved.

To become self confident, there are many useful steps. The first of these is "self talk." It has been shown through extensive research, that self-talk for students who suffer from test anxiety, should be well monitored, in order to make sure that it contributes to self confidence as opposed to sinking the student. Frequently the self talk of test-anxious students is negative or self-defeating, thinking that everyone else is smarter and faster, that they always mess up, and that if they don't do well, they'll fail the entire course. It is important to decreasing anxiety that awareness is made of self talk. Try writing any negative self thoughts and then disputing them with a positive statement instead. Begin self-encouragement as though it was a friend speaking. Repeat positive statements to help reprogram the mind to believing in successes instead of failures.

Helpful Techniques

Other extremely helpful techniques include:

Self-visualization of doing well and reaching goals
While aiming for an "A" level of understanding, don't try to "overprotect" by setting your expectations lower. This will only convince the mind to stop studying in order to meet the lower expectations.
Don't make comparisons with the results or habits of other students. These are individual factors, and different things work for different people, causing different results.
Strive to become an expert in learning what works well, and what can be done in order to improve. Consider collecting this data in a journal.
Create rewards for after studying instead of doing things before studying that will only turn into avoidance behaviors.
Make a practice of relaxing - by using methods such as progressive relaxation, self-hypnosis, guided imagery, etc - in order to make relaxation an automatic sensation.
Work on creating a state of relaxed concentration so that concentrating will take on the focus of the mind, so that none will be wasted on worrying.
Take good care of the physical self by eating well and getting enough sleep.
Plan in time for exercise and stick to this plan.

Beyond these techniques, there are other methods to be used before, during and after the test that will help the test-taker perform well in addition to overcoming anxiety.

Before the exam comes the academic preparation. This involves establishing a study schedule and beginning at least one week before the actual date of the test. By doing this, the anxiety of not having enough time to study for the test will be automatically eliminated. Moreover, this will make the studying a much more effective experience, ensuring that the learning will be an easier process. This relieves much undue pressure on the test-taker.

Summary sheets, note cards, and flash cards with the main concepts and examples of these main concepts should be prepared in advance of the actual studying time. A topic should never be eliminated from this process. By omitting a topic because it isn't expected to be on the test is only setting up the test-taker for anxiety should it actually appear on the exam. Utilize the course syllabus for laying out the topics that should be studied. Carefully go over the notes that were made in class, paying special attention to any of the issues that the professor took special care to emphasize while lecturing in class. In the textbooks, use the chapter review, or if possible, the chapter tests, to begin your review.

It may even be possible to ask the instructor what information will be covered on the exam, or what the format of the exam will be (for example, multiple choice, essay, free form, true-false). Additionally, see if it is possible to find out how many questions will be on the test. If a review sheet or sample test has been offered by the professor, make good use of it, above anything else, for the preparation for the test. Another great resource for getting to know the examination is reviewing tests from previous semesters. Use these tests to review, and aim to achieve a 100% score on each of the possible topics. With a few exceptions, the goal that you set for yourself is the highest one that you will reach.

Take all of the questions that were assigned as homework, and rework them to any other possible course material. The more problems reworked, the more skill and confidence will form as a result. When forming the solution to a problem, write out each of the steps. Don't simply do head work. By doing as many steps on paper as possible, much clarification and therefore confidence will be formed. Do this with as many homework problems as possible, before checking the answers. By checking the answer after each problem, a reinforcement will exist, that will not be on the exam. Study situations should be as exam-like as possible, to prime the test-taker's system for the experience. By waiting to check the answers at the end, a psychological advantage will be formed, to decrease the stress factor.

Another fantastic reason for not cramming is the avoidance of confusion in concepts, especially when it comes to mathematics. 8-10 hours of study will become one hundred percent more effective if it is spread out over a week or at least several days, instead of doing it all in one sitting. Recognize that the human brain requires time in order to assimilate new material, so frequent breaks and a span of study time over several days will be much more beneficial.

Additionally, don't study right up until the point of the exam. Studying should stop a minimum of one hour before the exam begins. This allows the brain to rest and put things in their proper order. This will also provide the time to become as relaxed as possible when going into the examination room. The test-taker will also have time to eat well and eat sensibly. Know that the brain needs food as much as the rest of the body. With enough food and enough sleep, as well as a relaxed attitude, the body and the mind are primed for success.

Avoid any anxious classmates who are talking about the exam. These students only spread anxiety, and are not worth sharing the anxious sentimentalities.

Before the test also involves creating a positive attitude, so mental preparation should also be a point of concentration. There are many keys to creating a positive attitude. Should fears become rushing in, make a visualization of taking the exam, doing well, and seeing an A written on the paper. Write out a list of affirmations that will bring a feeling of confidence, such as "I am doing well in my English class," "I studied well and know my material," "I enjoy this class." Even if the affirmations aren't believed at first, it sends a positive message to the subconscious which will result in an alteration of the overall belief system, which is the system that creates reality.
If a sensation of panic begins, work with the fear and imagine the very worst! Work through the entire scenario of not passing the test, failing the entire course, and dropping out of school, followed by not getting a job, and pushing a shopping cart through the dark alley where you'll live. This will place things into perspective! Then, practice deep breathing and create a visualization of the opposite situation - achieving an "A" on the exam, passing the entire course, receiving the degree at a graduation ceremony.

On the day of the test, there are many things to be done to ensure the best results, as well as the most calm outlook. The following stages are suggested in order to maximize test-taking potential:

Begin the examination day with a moderate breakfast, and avoid any coffee or beverages with caffeine if the test taker is prone to jitters. Even people who are used to managing caffeine can feel jittery or light-headed when it is taken on a test day.

Attempt to do something that is relaxing before the examination begins. As last minute cramming clouds the mastering of overall concepts, it is better to use this time to create a calming outlook.

Be certain to arrive at the test location well in advance, in order to provide time to select a location that is away from doors, windows and other distractions, as well as giving enough time to relax before the test begins.

Keep away from anxiety generating classmates who will upset the sensation of stability and relaxation that is being attempted before the exam.

Should the waiting period before the exam begins cause anxiety, create a self-distraction by reading a light magazine or something else that is relaxing and simple.

During the exam itself, read the entire exam from beginning to end, and find out how much time should be allotted to each individual problem. Once writing the exam, should more time be taken for a problem, it should be abandoned, in order to begin another problem. If there is time at the end, the unfinished problem can always be returned to and completed.

Read the instructions very carefully - twice - so that unpleasant surprises won't follow during or after the exam has ended.

When writing the exam, pretend that the situation is actually simply the completion of homework within a library, or at home. This will assist in forming a relaxed atmosphere, and will allow the brain extra focus for the complex thinking function.

Begin the exam with all of the questions with which the most confidence is felt. This will build the confidence level regarding the entire exam and will begin a quality momentum. This will also create encouragement for trying the problems where uncertainty resides.

Going with the "gut instinct" is always the way to go when solving a problem. Second guessing should be avoided at all costs. Have confidence in the ability to do well.

For essay questions, create an outline in advance that will keep the mind organized and make certain that all of the points are remembered. For multiple choice, read every answer, even if the correct one has been spotted - a better one may exist.

Continue at a pace that is reasonable and not rushed, in order to be able to work carefully. Provide enough time to go over the answers at the end, to check for small errors that can be corrected.

Should a feeling of panic begin, breathe deeply, and think of the feeling of the body releasing sand through its pores. Visualize a calm, peaceful place, and include all of the sights, sounds and sensations of this image. Continue the deep breathing, and take a few minutes to continue this with closed eyes. When all is well again, return to the test.

If a "blanking" occurs for a certain question, skip it and move on to the next question. There will be time to return to the other question later. Get everything done that can be done, first, to guarantee all the grades that can be compiled, and to build all of the confidence possible. Then return to the weaker questions to build the marks from there.

Remember, one's own reality can be created, so as long as the belief is there, success will follow. And remember: anxiety can happen later, right now, there's an exam to be written!

After the examination is complete, whether there is a feeling for a good grade or a bad grade, don't dwell on the exam, and be certain to follow through on the reward that was promised...and enjoy it! Don't dwell on any mistakes that have been made, as there is nothing that can be done at this point anyway.

Additionally, don't begin to study for the next test right away. Do something relaxing for a while, and let the mind relax and prepare itself to begin absorbing information again.

From the results of the exam - both the grade and the entire experience, be certain to learn from what has gone on. Perfect studying habits and work some more on confidence in order to make the next examination experience even better than the last one.

Learn to avoid places where openings occurred for laziness, procrastination and day dreaming.

Use the time between this exam and the next one to better learn to relax, even learning to relax on cue, so that any anxiety can be controlled during the next exam. Learn how to relax the body. Slouch in your chair if that helps. Tighten and then relax all of the different muscle groups, one group at a time, beginning with the feet and then working all the way up to the neck and face. This will ultimately relax the muscles more than they were to begin with. Learn how to breathe deeply and comfortably, and focus on this breathing going in and out as a relaxing thought. With every exhale, repeat the word "relax."

As common as test anxiety is, it is very possible to overcome it. Make yourself one of the test-takers who overcome this frustrating hindrance.

Special Report: Retaking the Test: What Are Your Chances at Improving Your Score?

After going through the experience of taking a major test, many test takers feel that once is enough. The test usually comes during a period of transition in the test taker's life, and taking the test is only one of a series of important events. With so many distractions and conflicting recommendations, it may be difficult for a test taker to rationally determine whether or not he should retake the test after viewing his scores.

The importance of the test usually only adds to the burden of the retake decision. However, don't be swayed by emotion. There a few simple questions that you can ask yourself to guide you as you try to determine whether a retake would improve your score:

1. What went wrong? Why wasn't your score what you expected?

Can you point to a single factor or problem that you feel caused the low score? Were you sick on test day? Was there an emotional upheaval in your life that caused a distraction? Were you late for the test or not able to use the full time allotment? If you can point to any of these specific, individual problems, then a retake should definitely be considered.

2. Is there enough time to improve?

Many problems that may show up in your score report may take a lot of time for improvement. A deficiency in a particular math skill may require weeks or months of tutoring and studying to improve. If you have enough time to improve an identified weakness, then a retake should definitely be considered.

3. How will additional scores be used? Will a score average, highest score, or most recent score be used?

Different test scores may be handled completely differently. If you've taken the test multiple times, sometimes your highest score is used, sometimes your average score is computed and used, and sometimes your most recent score is used. Make sure you understand what method will be used to evaluate your scores, and use that to help you determine whether a retake should be considered.

4. Are my practice test scores significantly higher than my actual test score?

If you have taken a lot of practice tests and are consistently scoring at a much higher level than your actual test score, then you should consider a retake. However, if you've taken five practice tests and only one of your scores was higher than your actual test score, or if your practice test scores were only slightly higher than your actual test score, then it is unlikely that you will significantly increase your score.

5. Do I need perfect scores or will I be able to live with this score? Will this score still allow me to follow my dreams?

What kind of score is acceptable to you? Is your current score "good enough?" Do you have to have a certain score in order to pursue the future of your dreams? If you won't be happy with your current score, and there's no way that you could live with it, then you should consider a retake. However, don't get your hopes up. If you are looking for significant improvement, that may or may not be possible. But if you won't be happy otherwise, it is at least worth the effort. Remember that there are other considerations. To achieve your dream, it is likely that your grades may also be taken into account. A great test score is usually not the only thing necessary to succeed. Make sure that you aren't overemphasizing the importance of a high test score. Furthermore, a retake does not always result in a higher score. Some test takers will score lower on a retake, rather than higher. One study shows that one-fourth of test takers will achieve a significant improvement in test score, while one-sixth of test takers will actually show a decrease. While this shows that most test takers will improve, the majority will only improve their scores a little and a retake may not be worth the test taker's effort.

Finally, if a test is taken only once and is considered in the added context of good grades on the part of a test taker, the person reviewing the grades and scores may be tempted to assume that the test taker just had a bad day while taking the test, and may discount the low test score in favor of the high grades. But if the test is retaken and the scores are approximately the same, then the validity of the low scores are only confirmed. Therefore, a retake could actually hurt a test taker by definitely bracketing a test taker's score ability to a limited range.

Special Report: Additional Bonus Material

Due to our efforts to try to keep this book to a manageable length, we've created a link that will give you access to all of your additional bonus material.

Please visit http://www.mometrix.com/bonus948/iltsapt to access the information.